Contents

Mahesh Thakur
QUOTES
Popular Prakashan
www.popularprakashan.com

Published by
Harsha Bhatkal for
POPULAR PRAKASHAN PVT. LTD.
301, Mahalaxmi Chambers
22, Bhulabhai Desai Road
Mumbai - 400 026

First Published 2021

ISBN: 978-81-948714-4-6

Cover painting: Ananya Banerjee
Design: Anjali Sawant

PRINTED IN INDIA
by Saurabh Printers (P) Ltd.
Plot No. 67 A-68, Ecotech, Ext. I
Kasna, Greater Noida-201306 (U.P)

Preface

In all my years of seeking the ultimate truth, I have come to realize that to experience the ultimate truth of the cosmos and beyond, all one needs to do is hold pristine thoughts throughout their existence. But this task is not easy, as physical life has already sucked us in and most of our time we spend seeking material possessions, our personal self and desires have taken over the 'I' and in doing so, alienated us from our purpose in life altogether. Our definition of our existence here on this planet has been reduced to survival, just plain survival. I am sure you too will agree to this truth, that somewhere within our heart we know that there is more to life than what we are subjecting ourselves to. In my moments of pristine clarity, I merely channelized that, and these quotes and powerful messages from the greater source flowed like a burst of fragrance and adorned the pages of this book.

Mahesh Thakur

Introduction

The Universe is an infinite place, within this infinity we are dealing with a finite existence; it is in the rapture of these finite ideologies where we have shortened almost everything about our own infinite existence.

From my humble beginning as a child in this world, I was never satisfied with the answers I got to my questions. My parents and teachers were amused at my questions but never managed to answer them. It could be that they hadn't attempted these questions themselves, or it could simply mean that they were satisfied with the answers found in certain revered texts. But I had decided, it will be the seeker within me which will not give up the search for these questions.

I hadn't understood then but my journey of understanding 'Self' had begun. Every question I searched was answered as time moved on, but not in ways our human mind is tuned to receive them. These answers were in the life force governing our existence. These answers were in the pulsating love of the universe which encompasses us all.

'Thoughts'... The origin of all conflict and the solution too. Thoughts are what empower us on a certain level and having a clearer picture about them can help solve many limitations about our outlook to life and in doing so tune us to that which is the infinite within our being.

Positivity, Confidence, Determination, Productivity, Direction of Self and Spiritual Knowledge are just a few aspects that will be the outcome once you read and indulge your mind in this book.

Most of those who have read and grasped the information in this book have benefitted on many levels within their consciousness and are today experiencing a freedom they never imagined could be possible. The clarity of their thoughts is the one reason for this freedom they claim.

So, be it about inspiration, motivation or spirituality, I have thrown light on these very subjects. There are 169 quotes written in simple language which I believe, will assist you in understanding yourself and improve your interaction with the world around you better.

It would also be much appreciated if you'll post a testimony about this book to help other readers notice it. Who knows; maybe that one testimony or review would help someone decide to read this book and might just change his outlook for a better tomorrow. Greater consciousness awaits you through these very pages.

Happy reading...

Acceptance, A Virtue

"Acceptance is a known virtue of the highest order in the spiritual realms! The testing ground is here on earth, this physical realm.

All of life's woes, pains and sufferings arise from the 'non-acceptance' of what your journey here is meant for.

Our non-acceptance is a vision about life we have created; it is very little of what we have understood about it. It is therefore just a perspective; a view from the stained glass of our thoughts and ideas!

Accept everything that comes your way and use the freedom of choice to learn and rise above events – for it's a virtue you must instill on the path to realization and enlightenment!"

Much love

The Creator's Vision

"He comes in ways unknown to many. Shall possess the being of a mortal to blend amongst you: How would you know if 'that' man who knocked on your door and asked for a piece of bread was none other than the embodiment of God Himself?

How have 'you' defined the carrier of light – and his greatness, in your assumptions?

I can't imagine this perfectly created world with all different forms of life; the immense beauty and colours not being visited by the creator Himself on a daily basis.

Or could it be that it is not much of a mystery if we assume that each one of us when we think of the creator, our eyes become the window for the creator Himself to perceive His Word."

Much love

Welcoming the Masters

"Many of the known who have attained true knowledge and wisdom of the beyond have guarded the secret only for the worthy.

Who then are the worthy? Can we consider ourselves so?

Man in all his understanding of his domain is but a fragmented reality of himself. His 'WILL' to 'DEFINE' everything and every event limits him to his basic instinct - 'Survival'.

Though survival is the primeval instinct, it is also what wears him down spiritually.

It is the rising above the survival instinct; it is in including 'Love' and 'Trust' in all your deeds towards oneself and others which carves a permanent stamp of worthiness in the eyes of the masters. It is then that the master approaches.

And 'HE' who awaits the Master does so with complete trust and faith not only in his teachings but in the ever resonating love which will protect him and guide him."

Much love

What is Mine?

"A good way to deal with daily confusions and stress is to ask yourself just one question: What is MINE? You will be amazed that after eventually answering all questions within your questions, you will arrive at the same answers all saints have arrived at, which is – 'When even this body leaves us at some point in time how can one claim anything to be connected to it?' Therefore enjoy this existence with this mantra on your lips and heart ALL IS THINE NONE IS MINE."

Much love

Finite Matter; Infinite Spirit

"In this universe of existence and experience it's 'matter' is what matters most.

But just above this realm of our known physical world the boundaries are infinite; to comprehend this, one must become One with the 'Spirit', the all knowing.

It isn't that difficult to become one with the spirit for our life force already is a part of it. One has to just become aware of this life force within ourselves.

Look around, touch, feel your surroundings and remind yourself 'IT'S ALL MATTER'! And your real self is not a part of it. Your real self is just experiencing it."

Much love

The Spiritual Personality

"Abilities define personalities. The ability to think logically defines one's intelligence. The ability to reason and understand minute emotional upheavals defines one's maturity. And the ability to accept unconditionally, forgive unconditionally, and love unconditionally defines ones spirituality - and this the most radiant of them all is also the one which transcends all time and space and nurtures one's intelligence and maturity.

Walk the path. Define your personality as a spiritual one!"

Much love

A Love Beyond Expectation

"To 'love' is most noble. Asking for reciprocal love is what mars the purity of it.

It is actually a deep sense of insecurity, and therefore the need of knowing that the feeling so pure felt by one has reached the other and if it has, it should resound back with equal force.

But when one channelizes the ultimate love of God, he becomes the carrier of the abundance of love within himself. He not only has realized what feelings you sent across; but somewhere because he basked in the purity of God's love he was responsible in invoking those feelings within you too.

Open your heart to the purity of love which transcends time and space, penetrates through your human consciousness and holds you warm within His shadow. Yes you too have the ability to feel God's love, just as you felt the same love for the other.

Love for no reason. 'Love' because love itself is the reason."

Much love

A Dialogue of Love

"I have questions – questions dear God, which need answers: Why did I miss a chance of good fortune so many times? Why was I given so much pain and suffering? Why was I always the one who lost out on love? My life would have been better only if you cared more for me, a little more dear God!

God Answers –

You are linked to one another like the metal rings of a chain which interlope with each other.

Your pain and suffering if felt by you is surely translated to the other and therefore the emotional burden shared.

You never walk alone in this life I say! And when you do feel alone it's simply because the 'Love' within you is being dimmed by the happenings around you.

But the loneliness felt within is never the exterior force. Its but your inability to fill your cup with Love; 'that Love' which is always resonating along your heartbeat – 'My love'."

Much love

The Time is Now

"How many have realized that time exists within time? A distant memory of your past can stir similar emotions felt 'then' if reflected upon! Or a feeling of great love if imagined upon correctly!

Our precious self's are capable of so much. Our determination and conviction is all what is needed to turn the tides in our favour.

So where do you begin one asks?

Right here. Right now. In the grand chamber of knowledge; in that dusty book called experience, which was kept away on the last shelf of your conscious mind.

Jog your memory or use your imagination.
YOU ARE ALWAYS ABOVE THE EVENT!"

Much love

Existence

"I have questioned everything and yet found no answers to many.

I have believed in much too much, but still have found no mental comfort.

I have done what must be done to the extent of all my capabilities, but yet there is a void within my being.

Why? I ponder while I gaze at the sunset: Why must it all end one day? While the blanket of darkness envelops the evening sky, the twinkling stars further my inquisitiveness.

Where do I really come from? When? When did I really come into existence?

Then is when the deep echoes of my voice consume my entire being, and it says – I have not entered this existence by sheer chance; but just like the stars and the moon above by a definite design!

If I didn't exist neither would this universe around."

Much love

The Child Within

"I have smiled at those paper boats which floated on the rainy water puddles; and waved a goodbye to the distant aircraft too.

When did I lose my true innocence to intelligence I wonder?

Was it when the loveliness of a tender heart and the honesty of my child within got compromised when intelligence defined pride?

Or when my little wishes were blown away with stark realities which people called 'Life'?

All in all I don't search for my desires to be fulfilled anymore. But I search for that contended child within; the child that attaches its true identity to simple innocence and pure love."

Much love

While You Were Talking

"1. **To Understand the World around Us:** Most of us begin life by 'talk', by asking questions about things, or why the world is the way it is, where we talk to open our 'understanding' and this is the best talk one can/should indulge in! Books help, sometimes an educational program and the most beneficial is a close association with evolved teachers, masters and guides!

2. **Where we Impart Knowledge:** All of us, each one of us has something to teach from our experiences which have made us gain a wealth of knowledge pertaining to what we do, or are doing! Mind you, it is not an easy type of talk for such talk can take you down an EGO sparring lane. So impart knowledge only and only when asked!

3. **Expressing Yourself and Talking about Others:** This is one of the most common and spiritually weakest talk one indulges in, showing how disgusted you are about situations, complaining, and talking about others; even listening to what others 'FEEL' about you or other people or situations.

Basically if it is 'not' gaining knowledge or imparting knowledge, every other category falls in this talk. And isn't it strange that it is this very 'talk' which robs us from finding peace and balance within!

So here are the three types of 'talk'. Be wise in choosing the type you indulge in. We have only that many hours attached to our lives and 'talk' is an important facet of life and living. ”

Much love

The Selfless Divinity Within

"Our human existence is a true lesson of transformation from the selfish to the selfless.

Every delayed action towards the selfless state of consciousness binds us in the drudgery- 'repeated torture'.

Our sufferings, be these mental, emotional or physical have their roots sowed deep in the delayed action of our selfless state.

It's more like a due date payment not made.

Evolution in the spiritual sense is finding your divinity. This is possible only and only when one practices being selfless daily.

All is His none is ours."

Much love

The Mental Fast

"Have 'nothing' to say sometimes.

For only in 'silence' will you absorb the real happenings around you.

For every time we pass a judgment or express a thought to another, the interaction itself occupies precious 'self analytical time'.

Like a mental fast give yourself SILENCE and unlock the hidden truths about yourself!"

Much love! Silence be!

About Balance

"A walk on a tightrope with balance beam on your hand is best compared to seeking 'pure happiness and focus' in living this life to its fullest!

Either side of the balance beam has a quality namely 'optimism' and 'pessimism'; and if either One gets your attention for too long, you will lose your focus and fall of the rope of pure happiness!

Take a step at a time! Weigh the pros and cons! It's the 'neutral' path which will help you get there! There never are shortcuts, only illusions of them beneath the tight rope you walk on called LIFE."

Much love

The True Being

"We've been the air one breaths;

We've been the fire that heats;

We've been the seas that tide,

And we've been that majestic mountain too.

The element to nurture is the fifth one in line, for which we have embodied the shell of Man.

But wait what do you know about the fifth element called LOVE? Ask yourself in your solitude. Is it your reason to find it in another? Or a journey to realize it and become 'Love' itself, the pure expression of your true being!

The consciousness of God is to be realized. And only through your true being it is said!

You've crossed all the elements as a consciousness and now awaken that which never slept – Your true being!"

Much love

Anger

"Ohhh! That all encompassing ANGER! That which controls your being: That negative force which you deem as a part of your nature is nothing more than fooling you to believing its 'OK'.....

It's ok; lose it!... It's ok to vent it out! But here is what I like to express.

It's never ok; and it will never be. Anger will consume you; that's the way it works. It starts at a level, then it roots itself on a firmer ground within your consciousness and then it wears deceptive clothing like pride and sometimes status. It makes you believe that you have the 'right' to get angry.

Though getting angry is common phenomena in all, it's also a subconscious trigger for depression! And 'That' is why one has to understand it!

You need not 'control' anger; but actually just look out for the things which trigger it! And those things which do, try and manage them! If you can't manage them, avoidance is the best way out."

Much Love ! Be at peace!

The Driver's Seat

"You have no right to feel bad for yourself or cry yourself in self pity.

If your analytical mind has managed to drown your Being beyond reason, surely it is not doing a good job for you!

People, problems, and situations which bring you down will always exist. But the person in your driving seat, who makes you think the way you do, should not do such a bad job as to bring down your self-confidence.

Remove this lousy employee. And replace it with your true identity; that which walks the path of purity and faith; that which has no ulterior motive to entertain your being with fresh positive thoughts; that who loves you first!!!

Cheer up. And spread happiness around."

Much love

Vibrations

"The basic fabric of this universe and our physical body are 'Atoms'; something which you'll have learnt in school. And the basic fabric of atoms rests on a vibrational charge.

Depending on the rate they vibrate determines their ability to form molecular structures.

Water, air we breathe, matter we touch, even our own skin are molecules. The point here that I am making is that every atom depends on vibration.

The vibration which is in total symphony and harmony is that of Love - that which can't be structured into atoms or molecules, only felt. And that feeling my friends, is what works wonders for our being in totality.

Increase the love quotient in your lives. The only way it comes back to you is when you give it out to the world and universe around."

Think about this! Much Love!

True Freedom

"I was asked today when in conversation with a person about the meaning of 'True Freedom'.

The word 'Freedom' by itself means different things to different mindsets.

Freedom to choose and be responsible for the choices you make have found popular acceptance among societies across the world.

But 'True freedom' is a little known something, often confused with the word 'freedom' itself.

True freedom is a state where you belong to no one but yourself. No belief in anything controls you.

Success or failures have no outcome mentally or emotionally for you.

You respect all others but never get carried away in their emotional bonding with you.

You can be alone and never feel alone because you will constantly be basking in the glory of GOD.

And tenderness, love and compassion are not things you have to strive for as these are the outcome of being in a state of 'true freedom' in itself."

Much love

Inspiration

"Inspiration is one side of an equation.

Friends, teachers, family, famous personalities and sometimes even books and knowledge about great men who have walked this planet inspire us.

But inspiration is just half of the conquest – half of the effort. Inspiration needs to form the complete circle where you find the reason behind everything you do; everything you stand for or believe in.

The other side of the equation is finding 'THAT' creative force in you which by itself inspires you, motivates you to achieve – not just to succeed in what you strive for but motivates you beyond reason to find the 'Truth behind this illusion of life'.

And this striving to seek, by itself, is a deep calling of your soul to unite with the great consciousness 'GOD', to unleash your creative self. Start believing in yourself.

Self inspiration is a path to enlightenment!"

Much love

The True Master

"The external image.

The followers that follow.

The publicity which highlights.

Are all for the 'making' of a false GURU.

He who 'inspires', He who 'Truly' guides, shall not possess powers to change your destiny, but will awaken that which is asleep within you.

He might just be among you, camouflaged like the dew drop which sits on a blade of grass unnoticed.

Take that walk through the garden of life, with the simple knowledge that 'he' who knows the truth will not reveal it but instead will guide me to experience it."

Much love

The Protection

"The other day I was feeling low and I didn't know why. I walked around in self pity; I walked alone in self doubt; my actions were fine; my intentions too. So why the dissatisfaction? Why the anguish?

It's often said when one's awareness is low, and a negative emotional comment from another reaches your ear, though not necessarily directed towards you, one tends to absorb it sub consciously; and that event starts to play out itself bringing you down.

If one has his awareness 24x7 pointed to his higher self, seldom shall such an event occur. It's not necessarily that God helped you out; but rather, it was your constant quest to seek him which protected you from the dissatisfaction within."

Much love

Love and Live

"Am sure most of us have asked these questions – Why are people who are in our lives there? Why do they come in our lives? Why do they leave us? Is it our choice? Or is it theirs? Or is it by the grand design called 'Destiny'?

Many popular books have been written on this, many views exchanged.

But in reality all these questions arise from the word 'Attachment' – a function of the ego. Being attached to someone is just a way of life. It is an expression of love. Or is it?

In this 'WAY OF LIFE' you too have to find a way to your destiny; your ultimate calling. The calling to self realization paving a way for God realization.

Be assured that all who enter or leave our lives do so to shape our outlooks, our viewpoints, our emotions, our understanding and THAT is what is required – not the 'person' in question but the event – the residual effect from the association with the person. All of these people whether you love them or not are like little gears in a clock, whose main purpose is to move the seconds, minutes and hours arms.

Life is surely designed to help you open up to a consciousness greater than you can conceive now in a human form. So till then, go with the flow. Love and live to your fullest."

Much love

The Unblocking of God Energy

"The kindest of them all, the one with benevolence in every action, purity in his heart and love in each gaze he sets upon the creatures of this living planet, needs nothing to prove his connection with the Almighty.

The Almighty has already taken over his being and is provoking his each thought to manifest in the upliftment of his fellow beings.

The supreme energy is that which flows in each and every living creature and gives it 'Life'; and can only be dimmed by the mentality one possesses!

So work towards kindness in your actions; in your words and in your approach to others, for it might just unlock a vision you have never experienced yet – that of the Supreme Being channelizing his power through you!"

Much Love

Rise Above Doubt

"A little belief, a little spark of conviction in God's love for you will save you the doubt and the corresponding mental agony of evaluating everything about it.

Before you even realized it he gave you parents to take care of you. By the time you grew up he had someone already destined to walk along side with you. (Recognizing that person was your prerogative as he blessed you with freedom too.)

And eventually he will also receive you with open arms when you reach his home.

Trust him above all else. He may not speak your specific language, but he always does speak the universal language of everlasting Love and Compassion.

So hold no boundaries, no reservations, no limitations, no assimilations, no prejudice, and no fear.

Be brave and just open your heart to love."

Much love

The Wonder of NOW

"Your inability to recognize the illusion of time is commonly referred to as 'boredom'. Beware of it, for in its garb is actually hidden the gratification of your senses!

Each of your senses has twin abilities: that of gratification and the other of 'wonder and awe'.

Think of it. You actually walk and interact with everything around that has been put through some source at some point just for this eternal moment called 'NOW'.

Becoming aware of this 'Now' via your senses will spark wonder and awe in all His creation.

God is everywhere; even in your breath!"

Much Love

I Love You

"If I were 'only' the ocean I would command the tides in your favour.

If I were 'only' the wind I would sculpt the mountain ranges in your image.

If I were 'only' the fire I would burn the ultimate desire of love in your heart.

If I were 'only' the earth you stood on I would record your every gracious footprint.

But I chose to embody you too, so I can see what you see, to feel what you feel; experience what you experience.

I am in you as much as you are in me. So don't question my love for you. As your existence, it is in itself the mark of my love for you."

Signed - God Almighty

The Nature of the Quest

"Bring me the thirst; take away the water! Give to me lit coal so i can set my foot on it! I fear not the pain and suffering of bodily nature, for I give not heed to my limited knowledge.

I speak to you, oh great consciousness. Call it a prayer from my soul if you must. I have surrendered my will on to you, for in my heart I have felt your presence!

I therefore request oh great Divine, help me keep my spirit heart open! Help me awaken the spiritual love to do so! I shall be by your side and channel your divinity through eternity."

Signed - A true Seeker

It Will Happen

"That one moment 'that' missed judgment, is what it took to change everything which came about because of it.

One will never 'know' or even understand the implications of one's own action it is said; till the outcome or event comes to focus.

Do you know that even this post that you are reading, has taken up some of your time from the Universe, and delayed an action which you might have been thinking of undertaking, and which in turn would precede another action and so on?

Not that you might have lost time, but possibly might have delayed your time to a favorable condition.

So here are the dynamics. Let it go if things don't work out according to you. The universe knows best."

Much love

Conquest of Fear

“Dealing with fear is actually what compromises most of our valuable time. Sometimes just understanding what you may achieve when you conquer fear, helps in facing life’s most challenging times. Here is another wonderful story I like to share with regard to fear.

In the middle ages, when trade started depending on sea routes, most trade routes used something called ‘horizon navigation’, as long as they could see land on the horizon, that was the distance they would sail out to the sea.

Remember it was the same time where many people believed the earth was flat, and one would at some point fall off the end.

At this time there were few sailors who conquered fear and left ‘horizon navigation’ and ventured deeper into the unknown sea, where there would be no land in sight on the horizon. The courage, the fearless approach and the faith is what finally got them to discover new lands and pastures.

Think about it, if they didn't have the courage to face fear or when their ship was rocking in those mammoth storms or they lost hope and decided to turn back, the fate of mankind would have been different.

You too 'the creatures of God', must face uncertainties and fears because I believe that at some level you too are shaping yourself. Just like the world benefited because of these fearless sailors, the people connected to you too are going to awaken to realities they have yet to experience because of your experience with life's challenges. ”

Much Love

New Hope

"It is in the morning, 'that beautiful morning', which brings hope in the form of rays through the mist covered mountains.

Those delicate dew drops which gently tip down from the tree tops.

That bustling downward water stream; the cool morning wind which rustles through the trees. The chirping musical sounds of the birds; all start to unify and play the grand orchestra of 'caring love' that Mother Nature has towards its creatures.

It's strange then, that how we miss this calling of truth which surrounds us all every day.

So here is a reminder; just a little reminder! Leave the baggage you carry of yesterday, as today is again filled with a new hope!"

Much love

A Rational Existence

"It's called 'influence' or the ability to turn ones thinking in a certain way.

And the most common form is the media. With its power of propaganda it can convert a lie into the ultimate truth and vice versa in a jiffy.

'Critical thinking', 'self analysis' and 'research' are the only tools one must depend on when faced with mass mentalities.

Remember, a crowd of people, no matter how large, need not be reacting to the 'truth', but to the one who has managed to convince them of it.

The path of seeking God also is similar. It requires you to break away from that crowd or herd mentality and approach the subject with 'Critical thinking', 'Self analysis' and last but not the least 'Research'. The path to God is rational."

Much love

A Basic Understanding of Self

"My understanding about things around, be it pain, pleasure, suffering or injustice, is merely a definition of collective thinking of humans by which at some point, 'I' have tuned into by ways of interacting socially with them.

Yes there are instinctive understandings of these outcomes too – but more often than not we are 'taught' to react in certain ways.

So at some point when the neurons in your brain are firing up reactionary outcomes to situations, buckle up and question – WHY?

A doorway to understanding yourself spiritually is to intervene in the passage of your emotions, not when you are calm and composed, but in the heat of the outcome.

Then the sparkle of your pure spiritual energy will be experienced. And you will steer yourself out of the situation with great ease."

Much love

The Symphony of Harmony

"Every little detail in this world is a symphony in motion. Stop the flow of a water stream and somewhere downhill a plant's or animal's life gets affected making them change course for survival; or they might just wither away and die!

Our lives are pretty much similar so to speak. We are either the cause of an event or the receiving end of it.

If you are running around in stressful strides every now and then, you are pretty much at the receiving end of events caused by others!

Stop! Take a breath, understand your place, and see if you can be a 'cause' of your own harmony!

A balance within is not that hard to find once we can determine the cause. Mostly if not surely, we are always REACTING to events!"

Much love

A Seeker's Insight

I am sad today.

Not because someone hurt me.

Not because I lost something of importance!

I am sad simply because I lost vision of the truth that nothing lasts forever.

I am but a mystery myself, walking amidst the deep forest of this world's chaos, with only 'curiosity' and 'love' within my heart as a survival kit.

Fear can elude me for a while from the truth, but not change my will from seeking it!

I shall seek today. I shall seek now, for sadness cannot rule my being forever.

Much love

Experience – The Teacher

"Change in one's outlook only and only takes place because of experience! Not others' experiences, but one's own!

'Experience' comes through only the passage of time. For example, I never knew what changes would transpire in my mindset and heart till I lost a loved one. The experience of losing a loved one translated into a deeper understanding of my life. Something no book or attending a lecture would give me.

So I say this: Don't rob yourself of experience and wish only for the good! (maybe a radical approach) but in all faith seek emotional strength to cope with the bad experience coming your way.

For ultimately the greatest teacher of life is EXPERIENCE. And that's what we are here for!"

Much love

The Building Blocks of the Aura

“Do you know ‘What you are?’ Not ‘Who’, but ‘What’?

A little understanding in this ‘realm’ will unlock a special attitude which you will carry with you a long way till the very end of your life.

Our bodies are actually a huge mass of atoms fused together; atoms which consist of electrons, protons and nuclei, and are spinning at great speed creating a ‘Vibration’. This causes an electromagnetic field to be created, which covers our entire body, Aura, then there are empty spaces between the atoms which are being controlled by your ‘being’ itself – this is the cradle of intuition and emotions. Where in deprivation of love in all its beauty, it can lower your magnetic field and expose you to physical and mental ill health.

Protecting this field of energy is actually the most important aspect of your being.

Being happy, being content, giving love, harmonizing, forgiveness – all are the actual building blocks of a very powerful electromagnetic field around you.

So keep your thoughts focused on the above. And magnetize your being toward perfect spiritual health!”

Much love

The Great Design

"**Time:** The actual separator between cultures, people and faith.

Your birth has been at a specific time and in a specific condition. Your nurturing and education shaped your beliefs. Your personality therefore was designed.

Think about it. If you were born a year before or a year after the conditions would be different. The people in your lives too – Just about everything. So if you didn't have control of what TIME you entered this existence, logic explains it as an outside force or we deem it as a part of the great design.

Everyone every single person in your life is there because of this 'Great universal design'. Your differences, your interpersonal relationships are all a part of it.

Blessed be everyone and recognize them all as spiritual forces; as souls who entered in this time just to interact with you. Look at them not with the eyes you do, but understand their purpose of being in your life too as a part of this great, immense, design."

Much love

The Book of Desire

"**Desires:** Sitting in solitude under a great oak tree, watching the river run ahead of me and feeling the wind deflect from the mountains just beyond.

I reflect upon my book of desires, studying every page of it.

I notice the similarities in every page, that of 'the correlation of contentment' – Contentment being an experience of happiness.

I shut this book, just as I shut out my desires, and question – Why must my contentment be found in 'Desires'; and if it must, why not desire the 'simply achievable'?

Why not desire to love unconditionally, give unconditionally and forgive unconditionally?

One may disregard and claim the above to be difficult. But compared to the book of desires you hold in your heart, it's the simpler way to contentment!"

Much love

A Walk Outside of You

"I tried to remember what all I was thinking and doing yesterday. But I couldn't remember much. So I thought, why not remember every single detail today, watch my mind think, and also my actions, so to reflect upon it tomorrow.

Just as I did become aware of my every detail, I noticed how insignificant things have started commanding my being.

And there was the answer why! Why I couldn't remember these details? It is because they were insignificant!

Most of our lives are spent on mostly insignificant things. These things or actions hold no long term value.

But try going out of your way to bring a smile of happiness to another, and more than the other person. You yourself will start recording those positive happenings you initiated. And these, my friends are the humble beginnings of a fantastic journey of eternal happiness. Rise above!"

Much love

A Reflection of a Spotless Mind

"Just like the reflection in the mirror or on a water body, the human mind reflects 'your' image and thoughts in the way 'you' perceive other people.

They may not be that bad after all. It could, just could be that you yourself have imagined doing the unimaginable if you were in their shoes.

Cleanse your mind. Cleanse your thoughts for a better co-relation with humanity."

Much love

Know What Matters

"I am at a loss of words sometimes. Though I know what I want to say.

The interpretation is what holds me back. Not that one has given up and surrendered.

You, in all your knowledge and experience must also develop the ability to recognize when an argument with someone you love must be put to an end. It is not that you are wrong, but after a point everything starts getting misrepresented, causing more harm.

In a loving relationship, the people involved must matter most. Never the event!"

Much love

Peace and Harmony – The Guiding Forces

"Wouldn't it be wonderful, just simply wonderful, if all profits made by the media covering negative events would go to the families of those very same victims being covered?

At least when we tune our TV sets, to that TV channel highlighting their misfortunes, we would not just be spectators but we actually would be helping by watching.

For those who don't know advertisers (cash-flow/income) only go where viewership is most.

Other than these, I recommend don't fill your life with negativity just because it's being highlighted. Remember someone somewhere is making big money on your vulnerabilities.

May peace and harmony be your guiding force."

Much love

Love Completes All

"The true romantic with the eagerness of the expression of the heart, holds no pride; nor hides himself behind the veil of materialistic power he possesses. To melt that heart he truly desires, his love, his honesty his compassion will come to his aid.

She will respond, not with her voice, but with her heavenly grace. Her approval will test the waters of commitment and straightforwardness. All she will desire will be reminders of pure love from thereon.

Man and women were created as a tandem unit. Their unison is meant to be and not necessarily through social status but through the invisible force of the 'heart'.

There is always a lesson to learn in love. And always, the unsung song will be 'That only LOVE will complete you'. So I say find it in the heart of another human or seek it in the heart of GOD!"

Much love

On Luck

"You have all the required knowledge to improve your life. You have this knowledge locked deep in your consciousness. You have tested these concepts subconsciously and have felt a great relief. But you called it 'luck' or just expressed it as having a good day!

You, in all your right are not just a human existence. You are but beyond the pages of this human form. You are a universal entity, 'A child of the stars'. You have the capacity and have read the minds of your foes and friends too. But you acted selfishly; selfishly only to validate and preserve your egotistical stature.

It was when 'selfless thoughts' had overcome your being in that momentarily subconscious spark you experienced a change of 'luck'. And the key to this master lock was 'divine intervention' which is found with a selfless heart! Only the selfless heart!"

Much love

Being Human

"What can I say? I need to immerse myself in this life and be 'human' as they say.

Am I still searching for the answer to this eternal question, or do I know what makes me human after all?

It's not just the ability to learn from our mistakes I'm sure; nor the ability to forgive. It is surely more than the ability to love selflessly I believe; and something also tells me it's all of the above and MORE.

Could being human mean in its true sense a 'realization' that as my human form ceases to walk this planet eventually, I would have actually ripened a greater consciousness of being one with God? And could it also be that all it takes for this consciousness to grow in its ripened form is to put our thoughts to this great universal being at least once every day?

I do think of him more than once daily; and it's in my ability to do this consciously. And that, my friends, is what I consider a pure definition of 'being human'!"

Much love

A Moment in Greater Consciousness

"A being so powerful that it encompasses the entire universe and constantly pulsates with the everlasting breath of consciousness in its entirety, has no single form; no definition of shape or structure. It is revered as the formless; a source of pure love.

What would it be to be like him? The formless! Would it be to enhance and stretch our egos to a precision of perfection, or dilute our egos altogether, and try and encompass love and humility, compassion and benevolence just to imitate him?

It is said that if you could infuse these qualities in yourself even for a moment, you would never turn back to human consciousness.

Just a thought to spend a second in."

Much love

The Language of Love

"Language and communication are the most powerful tools that one can hone. The basic language understood by all is that of LOVE.

The completion of total communication in the form of love is understood by all as COMPASSION.

I always wondered if one understood the language of the smallest of living beings from the animal kingdom around them, would one ever harm them."

Much love

Awaken into Infinity

"I shall let my mind wander into the abyss to see if it can reach the helm of creation. I fear not what I may encounter, as I am sure to discover a probable explanation for fear too.

The twinkling stars have a story to tell. So does the entire unseen universe, as infinite as it is. In hindsight, there are so many finite things we deal with here in our existence on this planet, a paradox if I may underline, for we belong to this very same universe – the infinite one.

And it's not necessarily a 'universe' but maybe many universes.

But what if, if the finite is the illusion, and the pure connection made with every living atom here on planet earth is actually an infinite interaction – an endless one!

I'm saying, I'm just saying, that maybe you are experiencing the infinite right now right here, but maybe not with the vision you are used to yet!"

Much love

Destiny and Desire

"Is it meant to be? Or is it in our hands to steer our destiny? Do I have a choice? Or should I just go with the flow of things? This debate clouds thoughts of so many alike!

But the real answer is much different than the question has itself imposed!

Are you in perfect balance or in tune with the spirit – is real the question. The answer thereof would justify the question.

Has it ever occurred to you, that what you desire itself is 'also' a part of the grand design? And thus achieving it consciously gives you the sense of being in control of your actions. Or carrying that feeling of success with you? This amounts to being in tune with the spirit by itself!

Unfulfilled desires is but being out of tune with the spirit; and carrying a burden of unfulfilled desires can never help you get back on track with tuning in to the spirit.

So start afresh each day. Let go of the old unfulfilled desires and feel the spirit set a fresh desire in your heart. It could be something really small and insignificant but listen to that voice.

Then go with the flow and carry the sense of well-being after you have consciously worked towards it."

More later

Find Yourself

"This is right. That is wrong. Being opinionated, politicizing events; trying hard to impress someone; hiding from the truth; making assumptions; then changing outlook. Talking of win-win situations all the time; getting angry about issues just for effect; then finding a resolve to make a point. THE LIST IS ENDLESS.

Do you find your personality hidden somewhere in this list? If so then remember that you have a long way to understand the real meaning of being one with YOURSELF! For as long as you are trying to win people or are being affected by them in some way or the other, finding yourself is close to impossible.

What good is finding yourself? Many may ask! The answer lies in the discovery itself!

Is it a 'must' to find yourself - as others may ask: For them, it's a definite 'yes' for they are following dictates of others for to long.

To know oneself is to befriend a great individual called 'YOU'."

Much love

Comprehend the Illusion

"It has been noted by learned and high thinkers that 'GRIEF' is the outcome of self inflicted thought patterns.

If you possess thoughts of 'belonging' and 'achievements' on a daily basis, then you set the pace of starting to believe in them more than the universal truth – that human life is a temporary physical experience and more an eternal one searching for the soul.

Concepts like the above, to let go 'daily' and that nothing really belongs to you, and that all is a 'moving film reel', etc, is sometimes hard to comprehend.

But try it. Let your physical eyes be a lens of a movie projector and view everything as a temporary event: And 'YOU' are actually experiencing an illusion of 3D reality!"

Much love

Seek Happiness

"**Dear wonderful people:** 'Be happy' for the feeling is the closest to the divinity each of you possess.

It's the outer shell of your soul. That which is radiating life in each one of you.

Ask for happiness. Seek happiness. Make another smile and see it reflect in your own image. Strive for this sensation on a daily basis. It's the genuine experience of your own divinity.

People who steal away your happiness must be avoided at all cost. And make a mental note of this, that 'as the constant of happiness will increase so will the unraveling of the true face of God' – like a giant jigsaw; all the pieces will fit perfectly to make sense of a universal truth which surrounds us!"

Much love! Happiness Be!

The Asking

"Every day I die a little and yet I don't know it.

It is not that sudden death which is the obvious you must fear or question,

but that which slowly chips away your dreams and your beliefs.

You take with you an experience of a day every night when you sleep.

What did you gain? What did you lose? What was the reason of pain? Why were you joyous?

A life not questioned is actually a life not realized!"

Much love

Call it God

"There is but so much one can put their attention on. It is but a limited commodity, trust me!

The only problem I perceive is that one is always lost on what to put their attention on.

Should one put their attention on finances, or on relationships? Should one go with politics or the current trend of recent events? Or maybe put their attention on the past or future?

The list is quiet endless. But your capacity to emotionally charge you up, or bring you down depends totally on this limited commodity.

Think about this. Read what I have written one more time. And just surrender and put your attention on something far more worthy, far more beautiful – the real love you are receiving from an unknown source in the form of life, your life, place your hand on your chest feel that heartbeat and thank this 'Force' – call it GOD if you must!"

Much love

The Outgrown Purity

"The pure have no concept of defined dictates, be it of money, religion or nations. They are known in the world as Children!

You too have been a child at some point; learned to walk and talk; learned to think and express. The conviction of your ideology was purely dependent on your exposure to life.

But what can't be written in books or taught otherwise is to look within yourself!

The uniqueness of you – the torch bearing capacity of God's image lies with you. Your ability to absorb His will and do His will is all summed up in you; in your consciousness. When faced with conflict, be the child. Be that child of God which holds purity in all it thinks and does, and see the resolve sooner than you can expect."

Much love

Manifesting Your Dreams

"I have given up. Given up on 'Trying'! For if I TRY, I am able to tell the difference between effort and comfort; and sure enough I will always seek the latter. To truly follow your dreams, to succeed in all you wish, there has to be no effort. You have to be in pure harmony and tandem with your dreams. You have to synergize your energy with that of your goal. You have to live it first by believing you have already attained it. And somehow the 'giving force' – the spirit of life – will always bring you there."

Much love

Benediction

"A good wish is also a 'Blessing'; a silent thought which transforms another's energies.

Wish along then. You too have that power to influence another. Your good thoughts for another might just improve theirs and in this grand circle of life be rest assured that the same energy will find its way back to you.

To receive love is to give it first."

Much love

The Healing from Within

"There are so many ways to see things I have understood.

And it is applicable to every event in our lives.

The more closely you look at a 'disturbing' event in your life, the more reasons for it come to light.

Because of the event if you hurt on the inside for longer than required, one must revisit the event mentally and view it from all angles, apply all reason once again, and conclude to blame no one – not even yourself. And this, my friends, is called healing from within."

Much love

Dream Your Way to Knowledge

"Staring at the night sky watching billions of stars gaze down at me.

The light from them, which has taken billions of years to reach the earth – to reach me – for this moment, just for this moment! So I can't help but question this expanse – this Infinity; this Creation!

I have asked and ask again: Where did it all begin? Why did it all begin?

Neither my intelligence, neither my beliefs nor my borrowed knowledge from another can truly convince me of the answer.

The spirituality embedded in this grand design are like fancy jewels which you still have not been able to put a value on.

Therefore, I close my eyes and surrender to deep slumber; and dream a dream!

With this great satisfaction that I too am a jewel, and the reason I live is because of the WILL of this great expanse."

Much love

The High Thinker

'High thinking' brings other important characteristic to your personality, which by default improves your social skills and blends you seamlessly with self confidence and compassion.

What is 'High thinking'?

It is your ability to work your imaginative skills to such an extent that you find hidden meanings of Divine love behind each event in your life.

Much love

Letting Go

“Letting go is an art mastered by some. And in its true sense, has nothing to do with any form of attachment. 'Letting go' is much to do with your EGO. That part of you which 'gets affected'.

A negative event which may occur, always drags you down on two fronts – the exterior and the interior. The exterior gets repaired faster than you expect because time has proven so over and over again.

But it's the interior, the Self, which one needs to address. Here you are alone and the only guidance is your bitter experience – hearsay of others, and the dictates of social and moral laws.

And even though every logic you apply, the solution is to get back at the one who caused the pain. Its 'letting go' which actually gets you the sweet nectar of rejuvenation emotionally.

The ability of 'letting go' is exercising your higher self. It is of training it to enter realms which are far beyond the confines of human limitations – Your true spiritual world!”

Much love

The Power of Imagination

"If we all died yesterday and were born again today, and if it happened collectively no one would notice – so explains logical thought.

You in all your greatness possess an incredible two edged power: That of love and the other of imagination.

We speak of 'love' and experience it in our own way. Imagination, on the other hand, is quite left to the explanation of text books and physiologist's interpretation.

But the power to transform; to give shape to, heal, and seek the higher consciousness all dwell here in the imagination of an individual.

You have survived the chaos and fear many times. So now let's try and imagine – imagine yourself alive today and everyday – which obviously isn't too hard. But now imagine yourself close to God as you read this; imagine yourself in all the beauty and grace you wish to and uplift yourself. Imagine your way!"

Much love

Evaluation of My Purpose

"Been seeing this world, and not just with my eyes; I have felt the pain but not just superficially. I have understood the chaos and it's not just with my mind.

The imbalance around is being caused by unprecedented greed, lust, vanity, anger and attachment.

And somewhere the machinery is a much undaunted selfish approach to everything around you.

I therefore resign from this human self every once in a while and seek a better outlook to life.

So in my solitude, when I am by myself, I evaluate a higher self – go by my own path so as to break my own limitations. I shall rise above I'm sure, for I have come here to survive – not just physically but spiritually too."

Much love

Money and Fame

“I have nothing against successful people. But I just wish that those who consider the successful 'Successful' keep their views to themselves; for somehow it highlights the LOSER/ENVIOUS quality in them.

If you really want to appreciate another person, then please do search for a certain quality in them which is beyond 'Money' or 'Fame'.

In reality the above mentioned 'money' and 'fame' are byproducts of being in the right place at the right time!

If you ever view the circle of life closely you will agree to what I mean.”

Much love

True Love for Another

"What do I deserve - I ask myself; how much of my existence do I owe to another? I ponder away.

The ones that truly deserve to be where they are today are always humbled by their loved ones. This is because it's the smile on the face of a loved one which is cherished more than any riches can ever adorn.

And the one who truly loves and loves the one, shall never weigh the happiness as against the gold that one gifts; but would hold the highest regard for the 'time' spent together."

Much love
To the deserving ones who value time above all else!

Intellect and Consciousness

"The study of spirituality arises from more of a need – a need to experience 'love' in its purist form.

The intellect which scavenges books pays close attention to lectures by great masters; or indulges in fasting or prayer, is still working its way to control the mind and its responses.

Consciousness on the other hand is what lies just beneath the intellect and just above the soul body.

The soul body carries the information of the entirety – the omnipresent and the omnipotent; and can never be comprehended by the intellect; only experienced by the consciousness.

This divinely pure place, namely your 'consciousness', can only be accessed through feelings of pure 'Love' for oneself, and selflessness for others. The word for this is 'universal love'.

If ever you seriously want to study spirituality you have to inculcate 'UNIVERSAL LOVE' in your being so you can tap into your pure self!"

Much love

To Give Without Asking

"There are times one needs to awaken to a proper social order, especially when things do not seem to be so.

But the game of blame changes nothing!

What really will work wonders is the 'acts of kindness', which we will do unto another and compel the one receiving to believe it was done for NOTHING in return!

Difficult? Yes! But to bring about change in a social system, each one of us has to make a difference; a little difference! So what are you waiting for – for someone to be kind to you first? The domino effect starts only when 'Acts of Kindness' are embarked upon by YOU taking the first step.

Remember, you are also a force the world has to reckon with!"

Much love

Transcend Time

"Those that have passed this world are permanent memories. The living are just memories in progress.

All is but a 'grand timeline of memory' waiting to take form as a temporary reality; those eventualities which will get embedded as permanent fixtures in the annals of time.

So look past the horizon of time once in a while, and let your true energy tune itself to the Universe. This is that 'Energy' which gave you an existence here in this world.

Do the 'unusual'. Break the monotony. Spread the desire to love unconditionally. And be a part of the grand change of consciousness that which has already started to take form through select sources – you being one of them!"

Much love

The Awakening

"As the day passes and as the time flows into an eternal abyss, you move ahead in spiritual quantum.

You left behind your experiences for others to learn from and made place for the inexperienced to take birth where you once stood.

Birth, childhood, youth, middle-age and old age has little to do with numbers; on the contrary, these must be used as yardsticks to measure up in God's Kingdom of eternal life.

Pride not yourself with youth; for every second there is but another younger born. Fear not the unseen realm of death; for eternity has always been by your side.

Awaken! Awaken! Awaken! You are but on a timeless journey of 'Love and Life'."

Much love

The Internal Jigsaw

"Most, if not all, have a vision of the world they 'PREFER' to believe in. But 'truth', more often than not, is far from our systems of belief.

But established belief systems work best for most people. So where and how can 'truth' ever have a chance?

It is said that the interpretation of the word 'LOVE' is man's greatest fallacy – it is a convenient means to an end, or a start of comforting thoughts; and this should never be understood as love.

This ambiguous emotion is mostly the reason for man's depression.

Search it not in others therefore; for the greatest act of love starts with the acceptance of one's own limited self. What then is your limited self? It is that part of you which feels incomplete without another person in it; like an incomplete jigsaw where the fitting pieces are in another person's hands. Accepting your limited self and completing the jigsaw within, through God's love alone, is what should complete you. For you are never incomplete as long as you welcome the divine power in you; and that is the complete 'Truth' by itself!"

Much love

The Point of Surrender

"When it is said, and it resonates aloud in your inner being that – All belong to Thee.

When it is proven beyond doubt; and when in your own moment of silence you know 'that nothing lasts forever'.

Why does the fickle mind resent it, and find pain in these same very words?

Could it be that your consciousness has not matured enough? Or could it be that you yet have to learn the real meaning of 'Surrender'!

Surrender includes your pains, your problems, your insecurities and doubts; along with every possession you claim yours to the Almighty!

Blessed are those who remind themselves of this truth every day. For being in the glory of God is always right here and right now."

Much love

The Opportunity of the Seeker

"It is the falsification of deeds in the name of righteousness and assumptions of success, which have created impregnable bubbles of ideologies.

The rest who consider themselves unsuccessful, different, radical, or for that matter, plain observers to the happenings around them are indeed the blessed ones. This is because a vision far greater than what is known is being matured within their inner being.

Seek not the external. Just learn to look within, into your own uniqueness."

Much love

Earning Happiness

"In one of my talks I was asked by a student which attitude is the best to attain for a quicker spiritual realization. He was quite amazed when I suggested that 'do away with competitiveness, and instill helpfulness instead'.

'But I will lose my edge if I do not compete,' he replied.

I asked him then if he knew as to what lengths he is allowed to stretch himself morally to attain success.

'As far as the law permits it,' he quipped.

Amazingly, when I asked him what he was doing in my lecture, he replied that he was finding more ways to succeed in life, and thought maybe spirituality could help!

For all of you, who think that spirituality will give you a successful life (monetarily), let me assure you it's not necessary; but yes, the happiness which is attained from opening up to a greater consciousness, has no comparison in terms of happiness attained from material possession.

That's why it is said the more money you equate your life to, the more the difficult you will find to relate to pure happiness and joy!"

Much love

A Clean Mind

"That first step, that little internal spark to do something; that something more than you normally would do, requires a clear mind.

Thoughts lead to action. Action leads to reaction.

If you want reactions of your deeds to be positive in nature, if you want prosperity, health and good wishes from the people you interact with, then remember, that all it takes, is your mind to feed your consciousness with good thoughts!

Keep your mind clean. And no harm will come your way."

Much love

The Abundance of Love

"'Needs' are very different from desires. But the greatest problem of today's world is that we can't tell the difference between the two.

Our society has created a blanket of illusions and made it compulsory for one to strive beyond one's capacity, 'SO' as to fulfill his or her desire. This is what they equate to 'happiness'. But in all this, we forget the basic need of 'oneself!' – That which is called 'Love'.

To be loved every moment, and to have so much in abundance that because you can't contain it that it starts to flow outward towards the others you interact with.

This basic need is overlooked and in doing so, man has let his mind be void of it for so long that other passions of the mind, such as 'anger', 'lust', 'greed', 'attachment' and 'vanity', have found their abode in the comfort of the mind. The mind now defends these passions by reminding itself – 'So what! Others behave in the same manner'! Or the classic one 'I am only human!'.

So beware when you justify the passions of your mind. Remind yourself that you need to seek love first to cleanse yourself, and then literally embrace the pure human consciousness. And a birdy has told me that on the path of seeking God, you will find abundance of love in every step you take towards Him. And he awaits you with open arms. Go forth. Now!"

Much love

Suffering and Pain

"Your wardrobe consists of many garments. Even though you may have a favourite outfit, you don't wear that every day. Similarly, our life has many faces; our nature, and our many moods. If you ask me personally, then even in our weakest hour we worry about many varied things, and never just one.

In this dynamic world, situations and things have a way of changing faster than the process of thought. It is wise therefore not to brood or be upset on the same issue for too long; for when we do so, it is called 'Suffering'. Suffering is when the mind locks itself upon a single problem, and blocks one completely out of life. This is much like losing your keys to your personal wardrobe and wearing the same outfit all throughout.

It is therefore in your hand as to come out of suffering, for in the quest for God's knowledge 'suffering is considered optional and pain inevitable'."

Much love

Emotional and Mental Nourishment

"Feeling emotionally well, and mentally fine also forms an important part of your over all 'DAILY' diet.

Ask yourself what you take every day for an emotional supplement and mental supplement. Never thought of it? Well, then, read on.

Emotional and mental needs are very delicate in nature. These needs reside deep in your heart, quite locked away from the outside world; and from your own conscious mind too. But sometimes, and for no reason at all, you find comfort in things you do or certain people you interact with. This then is the daily supplement for you.

This is what you need to devote some of your time to. If you are not finding comfort in the things you do or in the people you are with - you are depriving yourself from mental and emotional nourishment.

Don't say it's not possible or give reasons otherwise - this life is yours and yours alone. Before you give your precious time to others, become a gracious individual by nourishing your true needs."

Much love

Finding Contentment

"People complain and wish life gave them a second chance. They wish and they wish and even sometimes pray for it. But I have known many who haven't even had a chance at all.

All it takes is to look around you and watch closely, and you will find so many who have never been given a chance. So, never complain!

Finding contentment is opening your heart to love!"

Much love

To Let Go

"When we need to understand the logistics and workings of pure spirit that which resides in all living and non-living, 'viewpoints' lose their meaning. On the contrary, to understand the workings of the spirit, we need to 'let go of all that binds'.

You see, the mind which is supposed to serve you in this life like a slave to your being, has found its way to becoming a master and in charge of everything about you. So, as long as you want knowledge of the spirit, you will not be able to comprehend it with the workings of the feeble mind only!

The best way to letting go of the iron chains which your mind has bound you in, is by 'ACCEPTANCE'. Accept everything about yourself and the life around you. Soon you will feel your heart fill itself with love, and will then start to experience a sense of extreme well-being. This is when the pure spirit of pristine knowledge and wisdom will flow into you."

Much love

The Reciprocal Love

"We let ourselves get pained by others. It's never the other way round. Look closely at yourself, why are you the way you are?

Here is what I think.

You, with all your intelligence and righteousness, have overlooked that simple facet to yourself – that which is 'love and trust'. This is actually the joker in your pack of cards (metaphorically); and you tend to play it with every hand of yours.

'Love and trust' are those special things which you have been blessed with; the more you use these, the less you will possess of it, that is, if it is not reciprocated.

So use this God given quality wisely. If you want an abundance of this sweet nectar, use it to love the Supreme Being unconditionally! God reciprocates 10 fold."

Much love

Time Traveller

"These are one of the most volatile timelines in which we all are in existence; where one faces ups and downs in every facet of life – be it financial, emotional, or the ritualistic guidelines of society and culture.

But extremities are actually opportunities, because it is only in the experience of the extreme, in which you shed the 'cover of comfort' of your 'thoughts and viewpoints'; it is also in the extreme conditions of life where you actually judge the spiritual qualities in yourself or in others.

Everything on this spiritual journey within your physical life is related to discovery of 'Self'. The sooner you realize this, the easier it will be for your consciousness to comprehend that you are actually a 'time traveller of a distant future', just re-living the excitement of discovering yourself and your connect with the Supreme Being."

Much love

Mysterious Ways

"I have heard many a complaint, that – 'I have been so good; why do bad things happen to me?'

The fact is that the goodness within you should never be looked on as a reason for you to be rewarded.

For the workings of goodness is purely to open up a new dimension in your thinking about why things are the way they are. It is the elixir, the sweet energy required to read the workings of God; and in doing so coming to realize His abundant love for you along with His Creation!

Be patient when faced with adversity; because God's ways are mysterious; but never against you."

Much love

The Five Pointed Star

"When we say 'peaceful', we are actually referring to being in total balance and in total control of our feelings. These feelings get rocked very often nearly every day on some issues or the other.

I urge you therefore to look at your life like the five pointed star. Each point measures the same from its core and is in equal distance from the other point; now understand that each point represents different priorities of your life, namely:-

1. Family **2. Career** **3. Health**

4. Finances **5. Personal relationships**

They should be given equal importance even though at times one may need more attention than the other. Remember, that if anyone of these priorities takes up more of your time or your mental thought patterns, then the others will get affected; and a domino effect will cause you to lose balance, and therefore peace.

Also don't take any of these for granted either. Let the five pointed star within you shine bright. Remember, that if one point is not working out the way you wish, the balance four are still there to shine bright for you!"

Much love

The Neutral Way

"I like to look at a negative and find a positive within. And it is pretty simple. For I know that no negative can sustain without a positive; and vice versa.

It is the neutral path which is the hardest to find, for it hides itself and only shows up when the two forces of the positive and negative fuse together.

I know I don't make sense to many readers with the above lines. But that is precisely what one must try and understand – that it is the neutral way where the secrets are hidden; and it's never in a bed of flowers or in a thorn bush either.

By being positive, you achieve control over emotions. By reacting to 'situations' you experience negativity. But by stopping and overlooking the impact of both these forces you to find the neutral. Then you find the wisdom and you find the knowledge. Think about it! Most answers lie within 'your' realm of existence."

Much love

Nothing is a Coincidence

"Someone asked me the other day - How come you never doubt the presence of the Supreme Being in your life? Couldn't all that happened to you just be a 'Coincidence?'

I didn't want to get into a further argument with him, for it seemed to me, he himself was struggling with coping with his equation with God and the happenings around him.

And that's what I consider important. Never make the topic of God an argument; for we ourselves are here to experience Him in all His glory.

Moreover, don't we all who follow the true path of God realization already know the golden rule – that 'nothing is a coincidence' in the first place? Everything is but a manifestation of pure spirit in your life, which makes itself obvious to nudge you toward the path chosen for you."

Much love

The Fraction of the Second

"If you really wanted to find justification and comfort in your thoughts, then stretch your thoughts to this.

You are but living on a definite timeline! When, where or how you will exit this timeline and slip into another will depend purely on how you view your co-relation with the Supreme Being.

It takes years and maybe life times of experience to understand God in all His mystery and glory. Once you do, it takes under a fraction of a second to slip into His pure consciousness.

It is all beyond time, space and matter. So to comprehend that glory, you have no yardstick of measure. But if you must it would be just the feeling of pure love which fills the void in your heart. That would be the connection; your true calling; your fate!"

Much love

Simplicity and Integrity

"Mind games are played by many. We recognize some but are unaware of the majority.

Safeguard your individuality and emotional integrity by simplicity in thought, word and deed.

Remind yourself daily 'that what matters is not what others think; but what you think about yourself'!

Don't fall in your value system by using means other than your true self just to impress another.

Seek the ability to find balance, peace and love within your own surrounding.

And lastly, remember that others can never give you Love the way you can 'LOVE' yourself!"

Much love

The Nature of Seeking

"In my time of silence in my moment of solitude, I burn with the desire of seeking 'anything'. For the whole purpose of seeking or yearning or wanting anything or something gets you, and you are, consumed by it.

Your actions and thoughts; your talk and reactions and just about all your sensory perceptions become alternate realities.

This alternate reality my friends, is what creates the divide between this world you live in and your physical body that you are meant to view this world from.

View the world; just view it without thoughts pertaining to your desires. View it without judging people around; without judging yourself in a positive or negative light.

And be ready to see; to view the spectacular spirit of God at work within his creation.

I have seen it and so will you."

Much love

You are a Star

"The real STAR is you.

Imagine a world without the media which keeps hammering the popularity of humans like you and brainwashing you to believe that media stars are better or more blessed or more gifted than you.

And you with all your capabilities intact, start believing 'that' which is being fed to you by this media. As a result of this, you start talking about stars; start copying them. Start adulating them to such an extent that you lose your own identity; your own individuality.

Let the creative force within you shine. These unique forces need not necessarily be associated with the media – with film, television, theatre, etc.

Let your creative force be about 'Love' and about giving love; about making another happy, and so happy, that the person in question makes you their IDOL, their STAR in their own eyes.

Here is wishing you all the stardom!"

Much love always!

Simple Harmony

"Take a moment to read if you are feeling low; disturbed.

Why give so much of your attention to issues and lose talk of people who really don't care about you? Also, why take the trouble to hit back at them? What difference does it really make if society around you disliked you?

Nothing, and absolutely nothing; for I have known people who survive dislike of others and yet are perfectly happy. In fact the same society cushions and fans their egos too.

It doesn't really take much to set things straight. For once you learn the art of ignoring and ignoring without 'Prejudice' you will not think of them at all. Leave getting back at them, for these very same people will come across in your mental framework as people who are just faces in the crowd of six billion.

If you must do something for yourself, you must work hard to find 'simple harmony' within your own being and live in the peace which comes from it."

Much love

Knowledge and Humanity

"A few fortunate know that educating oneself, learning new skills, graduating, mastering and involving one's intelligence in any subject has little to do with monetary success, but more for the 'Love' of knowledge itself! It is unwise therefore to think of education as financial freedom, even though that freedom is a byproduct of it.

'Knowledge' gained ultimately translates into spiritual awakening, with 'Humanity' being the byproduct of it."

Much love

Choices We Make

"A very interesting thesis was once conducted at a reputed university. A bunch of scholars were asked if they prefer a £250,000 job where all their peers also received the same amount in the company; or a £180,000 job where their peers received much less than them in the same company obviously depending on their job profile. The result was quite astounding no one wanted the 250k job but preferred to be above their peers even though it meant lesser salaries.

The thesis conducted was aimed at human interaction vis-a-vis intelligence applied on specific decision making skills.

The answer was simple human intelligence excels on basic feel good emotions. One needs to be above their peers to feel successful. It's like the ones you hang out with set the standards for you.

The conclusion to this thesis was improving your life by making choices of being in the right company.

It is noted that we have the choice to feel better about ourselves by choosing the right company. Just because you have been interacting with specific individuals all your life and complain you don't have time doesn't mean you can't seek better, take out time for yourself first. Then the next step is to invest it in the right company, the right people for you."

Much love

Words are Just Words

"Some things must be said; and sometimes nothing must leave your vocal cords.

The true seeker knows that words after a point are just words chasing words. You never needed words when the morning rays which brushed through the morning dew drops warmed your pillow gently just to wake you up! You never needed words when the sun slowly set and gently bought the night sky in your vision just for you to count the stars.

Words are for those who can't see, who can't feel, who can't pray the silent prayer of love.

Words are just words and only words for those who still need to experience the glory of creation.

'This is just a poetic justification in my solitude I often wondered! The truth is around us in the form of creation by itself. And we have but a garbled vision of it.' "

Much love

Recognize Love

"Let your mind wander and seek answers to your existence.

Evaluate your answers against the backdrop of love that you give to others and the love you receive from others. And for all you know, maybe it's this very factor which keeps your heart beating, keeping you alive and well; happy and content.

It is said that the spiritual 'winds of love' is what binds all humanity together.

It's the never ending imagination of the creator which has 'already' empowered your imagination to seek love to give love; and for you to feel His love always. Sometimes these currents of pure love manifests in your life at certain points just to protect you and put you back on track of seeking your higher self, recognizing that this love is in your hands."

Much love

A Celebration of Life

"I had a dream of loneliness and despair. The rejection of others pulled at my heart strings. My desires of success were slowly floating away into the abyss. I was a loser, and I knew it, for the world around me imagined me so.

But I awoke from the deep slumber just as the sun dawns on us every day. I looked out and saw a new day; a new beginning. Maybe I had no direction to follow. But I had looked at the distant horizon which proved to me that heaven and earth met somewhere. Where was this heaven? What was this place? I put this in perspective and sighed is relief.

As my dreams and reality meet somewhere, someplace, that place or situation is not for my ability to only react, for surely that place or situation is for me to act upon too!

The strength I derived by making a 'decision' even if it was a flawed one, gave me reason to smile, for I proved to be unique. In this uniqueness there was 'me'; a me far from others thoughts and imaginations; a 'me' designed by a Creator to think on my own, to act upon on my own; a 'me' to love and cherish today and every day."

Much love

Forgive All

"Mistake not the grudge you hold as something to pride upon, as it is the cancer which eats your very being alive.

Of all the virtues I therefore prefer to see forgiveness in others. Forgiveness sits atop the pyramid of life and beneath it – kindness, harmony and charity.

'Forgiveness' should be understood as a complete act in itself; and is never conditional. Forgiveness is the beginning of a self healing process. So let go of those timeless grudges you've held so long.

Let the kindness within you guide you harmoniously towards a blessed charity. 'Forgive' and pave your way to an excellent spiritual health!"

Much love! Blessings be!

The Magician in You

"It's magical – that which touches another's heart.

You would wonder why a stranger was good to you; and because of it you will walk with that elated feeling within you. Maybe carrying that good vibration just so you can pass it on to another stranger who in turn might just carry that goodness you set of within him for sometime more till it reaches another.

'It's magical' – the goodness within each one of you. You have the power to make another feel good about himself; and in doing so feel the power of LOVE within you by itself.

Practice some magic daily. Trust me, you all are magicians and can always create that 'Awe' and 'wonder' in another's eyes by your gestures of kindheartedness and goodness."

Much love

The Right Words

"Words hurt. You've known so. You've felt it so especially when someone you love speaks out hurtful words, it drops on you like a ton of bricks.

But words are magical too. Encouragement, positivity and upliftment of spirit is also what they can inspire in others. Words play an important part in our spiritual, mental and physical well-being too.

But remember, that when you think and talk in a negative fashion about others or about particular situations, a lot of negative residue is left in you. You might not know it but the damage it has caused will reflect somewhere down the line.

We are creatures of Love. The only things that affect our well-being are things which are contrary to love."

Much love

Be Happy

"I have seen people long for commitment in relationships and financial security to such a great extent, that they become completely vulnerable in their quest for it; and more often than not, land themselves in great agony. From there on, their lives are filled with resentments and pain simply because they feel they have been victimized.

The goal of life, if evaluated, must not be against the back drop of 'Happiness'. One must not attach this greatest joy to achievements set out by yourself or by those who have unknowingly influenced you.

Let happiness prevail in your life like the constant fragrance of love which you experience from little nothings. And the rest of the goals will be achieved faster than you can ever imagine."

Much love

Lessons Within Ego

"A person's ego is generally a muddled up version of their single minded perception of the God created world around them. Our conflict with egotistic people also arises out of the very same fabric which we have painted of the world around us.

If ever you want to look beyond the person and make peace with such a one, search not the qualities in them which may comfort you. Seek the life force which is powering this very same soul, this ego, which in turn is interacting with you. Search the lesson which the creator is sending through them for you to unfold. Seek the creator himself in their being.

This is the first step of fine tuning yourself with 'Universal Love'."

Much love

Lady Luck

"Do a positive deed, so as to create a positive memory each day and reflect upon a past one too. Let the negativity you have picked up over time get diluted by this act alone, and see how your life and all your endeavours thereof attract the other side of positivity – 'LADY LUCK'."

Much Love

On the Nature of Growth

"We grow every second in thought, emotion and spirit. When we say we have grown, we have understood and overcome our limitations and moved on; moved ahead to explore new dimensions within us and beyond. The old 'us' died along with those old conflicts which held us back emotionally and mentally, and a new 'us' is born in ideas, and within new dimensions.

So, in conflict and adversity is when your ego dies, thus creating a void which fills up by the love and knowledge of pure spirit, which in turn awakens your consciousness as a pure being of light.

So this you must know, that your immortal self is being born each second in you as you understand yourself as consciousness.

So fear not to leave your ego behind; for as you do, you are awakening in pure consciousness."

Much love

Born of Love

"It's not difficult to learn righteousness, or to give lessons of justice to others. This is because both these two qualities of righteousness and justice are highly prevalent in law books of the society's we live in.

What is of difficulty is to teach or to learn lessons of pure love. This is because windows of opportunity regarding love very seldom present themselves.

So here is what I say. When an opportunity to reach out and express love to someone who needs it shows up, go forward and play the part of the angel who wields the power to give love!

You have it in you; for you are born out of the same material God created this universe with – 'Love'."

Much love

Transdimensional Consciousness

"We all know and understand the three dimensional world we live in. But within this world, there exists other dimensions which we can't possibly experience with our human eyes. We therefore have to rely on our sixth sense.

The skill to open up to your sixth sense, that 'subtle' sense, can only be achieved through 'surrender'. When we say surrender, it means 'purely accepting a greater power beyond your control'. That power which knows all, which encompasses all; that power which is overseeing everything in this very instant.

Through practicing the art of surrender and acceptance daily, other dimensions will start to come into focus – slowly but surely!

This is the next level of experience beyond your human self, and just a baby step into the multidimensional God worlds. Look back just to enhance your comprehension of your own existence that you yourself started out as a single cell organism and have made your way into human consciousness."

Much love

Absolute Freedom

"When you walk the path to self discovery, freedom will be the byproduct: Freedom of thought and expression. Along with freedom you will also learn discrimination, so that you can use your power of choice wisely!

Then when you start making choices – choices which seem difficult, you start carving out a destiny for yourself and those who believe in you.

So if you feel your life is going nowhere, remember it is then time to break away from the routine comfort of the way things are and take control in the driver's seat! You always, always will find freedom in doing so, and the choice is yours! Come forth and experience your freedom! Take the plunge to self discovery!"

Much love

Love – The Ultimate Force

"The saints and the greats, the wise and mystics have all emphasized on one word – 'Love'. The meaning of it is found in myriad of texts written all over time. The interpretation of it has also been used by religions to express what God actually is.

But to put this word to use in our daily life, you must understand the word differently. 'Love is a Force', and a very powerful one too. It can attract knowledge and open up your consciousness to a greater understanding of self and beyond!

When we express ourselves to others by being kind or considerate; helpful or just wishing them well in silence, we are working with the attributes of this force and building a solid ground for our awareness to open.

On the other hand the complete opposite of 'Love' is 'Fear' and its attributes we are all aware of. Anger, jealousy, hatred, prejudice – the list is just endless.

Love as a force always resides in the present moment. Fear always attaches itself in the future or past. By this we mean that we will hold back because of a past bad experience or hold back because the future is unknown.

Our mind and mentalities will never comprehend 'Love as a force' and the amount of power it can wield to help us grow in knowledge and spirit. The only way to comprehend this is to work with the attributes of love by just letting go of the fear! ”

Much love!
May the force of love be with you always.

Open your Mind

"From 'Perception' to 'Interpretation' is where the root to conflict lies. The barbed wire around prejudice is actually a self mockery of old rusted ideologies.

To open your thoughts and to let the flow of positive energy flow outwards towards every living being belongs to no specific religion. It's the basic 'capability' of every man. Open your mind."

Much love

The Knowledge Within

"For a moment I imagined that I encompassed all the wisdom of the universe, and the flood gates of pure love just filled my being like an overflowing cup; it then left my being pulsating outwards all that which was alive.

Regard your imagination. It can create the most beautiful illusion and propel you towards a truth far beyond the realities which we consider impossible.

It is said that all there is to know is already there locked within your being. You are just not aware of it yet. You are but asleep consciously to a truth which is waiting to unfold.

You are 'that' which is being imagined in this instant by a power greater than your feeble mind can conceive. Tune into it. Your existence has not happened by chance. It is by a definite design!"

Much love

The Experience of a Million Suns

"You are connected with the spirit of God through an unseen force. This spirit of God is actually a counterpart to your existence by itself. And you can see, it works only when you capture the image of God and His attributes in your being.

When you truly desire something, and there is a greater good for that event to take place, close your eyes and surrender yourself to this spirit of God.

The manifestation of the event requested will pan out within this illusion of time. And only then will you come to realize that what you asked for was too less. It was but just a point of view – 'Your view' which you wanted to experience. The nectar of God knowledge is the brilliance of a million suns. And you just played with a spark. The spirit of God walks with you every second and where you are now, how you are now is best chosen for your spiritual unfoldment."

Much love

Humility within Spirituality

"We in such audacity go about judging others and their beliefs feeling that if only they 'followed' what we knew, their life would be so much better. In all reality their lives might just be better, far better. But maybe 'You' are not aware of it!

So when we call ourselves 'Spiritual' we must understand we have just let go of everything that gives us the feeling that our knowledge or way of life is 'Superior'. That is why spirituality cannot be preached. It finds a subtle entry in your heart and makes a permanent abode there.

The long winding road to becoming Spiritual is finding humility in oneself."

Much love

Know What Love Is

"One of the most mysterious energies I have encountered is the one between two individuals who are emotionally involved in a committed relationship with each other. We refer this to this energy as 'Love', but in all honesty it's more than that.

You get connected with persons on a very psychic level. You can unknowingly be doing things which you know will please your partner. Sometimes, you may even consciously be doing things to please the one concerned, even though it doesn't really make you happy, because in reality all what the heart desires is truly to feel pure love; a sense of knowing that the one you sacrifice so much for 'appreciates' your efforts.

But sadly, this mysterious energy is the cause of much heartache.

Tweak this mysterious energy a bit and search not for reciprocity. Open your heart a hundred fold – a thousand fold if you must. Love like there is no tomorrow in this radiant life of yours, to feel the purest form of love. You will have to give it till you feel it."

Much love

Goodness – The Eternal Guide

"The capriciousness in every man has lead to a state of total degradation. His will has been surrendered but to a monetary confinement. All he does, must be rewarded with a payment which he can see swell in his bank account. How then, can he explore his true intelligence, his true being?

The functioning of your mental self uses two basic methods to perceive the world around – one of compartmentalization, and the other of definition.

If every opportunity to change oneself and open the gates to a higher consciousness starts resting purely on the definition of 'monetary gain' where even doing a certain good needs to have a tangible outcome. Such is how the purpose to do good itself stands defeated!

So let go of all definitions. Do not compartmentalize, or try to give structure or reason for doing good. It is the only way to experience your true identity, your true intelligence, your true being. The goodness in you is your guiding light for the eternal journey within!"

Much love

Finding the Flow of Pure Knowledge

"One of the principal reasons you have a human embodiment is '_______'.

The arguments and beliefs put forward on this topic are so varied that it has left marks on each individual's perception and faith.

I for that matter have understood this that something within us lives on; imprints of distant memories and unfulfilled desires. Even the sadness and joys of the life just lived are recorded somewhere in our mental magnetic field.

But the pure spirit which powers your being pumps life into your heart, has to complete the full circle.

Your existence (life) started out in a blank mental state for you to enter the pure spirit worlds beyond physical death. The mental magnetic field too has to be reset; all energies neutralized, and your perception from the 'I' to a state of being which would be the all encompassing consciousness which perceives the awakened state, the sleep state, and the cross over state as a constant dream state.

So I say this: pure knowledge flows in when you experience the constant dream state within. Maybe this is what I experience, imagine and just share. Who knows? Or maybe I do."

Much Love

The False Enclosure

"Your surroundings are but a counter effect of your thoughts, just as you will it first to move from one room to another of your house, you have to also 'Will' it first to change your surroundings.

Nothing on the exterior ever changes by itself.

Concentration along with calmness produces 'the' desired effect and that little window of an idea which pops right open after you achieve your concentration along with calmness in the face of adversity is the stairway or the road map of your 'Will' taking form. Now all you have to do is move the physical muscle and change your surroundings.

Don't let your surroundings control you. You after all are experiencing your surroundings. Your surrounding is not experiencing you!"

Much love

The Value of Encouragement

"I may not have mastered emotions yet, but what I am about to say does hold true in my experiments with emotions:-

Encouragement is nourishment for the soul. Everyone needs emotional support. No matter how powerful or successful they may be, all have their weak moments. To inculcate the habit of encouraging your loved ones no matter how simple their task may seem to you is another way of giving love. Be generous with your words to those who need it and feel their love reciprocated tenfold!"

YOU CAN DO IT!!!

Much love

Quest for Compassion

"Your past achievements or laurels on how 'good' a person you have been holds no value in the present moment.

So advertising your 'Goodness' as a quality is plain foolishness, because the truth is that everybody has been good at some point in their lives.

But I have seen many who want to take credit for a good deed they have done in the 'PAST' to such a great extent that they have actually just become a ball of negative energy.

These very same people are left with just words which seem more like excuses, for they have lost the ability to put their spark of being good in their lives completely.

If you recognize this as your own character flaw fix it immediately. Being compassionate is the requirement of the hour. Awaken the goodness in you; start each day with a thought that 'something good must be done today', and before you know it you would have created a better world by doing so."

Much love

Freedom from the Negative

"It is very simple to know if a person is physically fit. Ask him to do some strenuous exercise and the results can be mapped accordingly. But how is one to know if a person is mentally or emotionally fit? Well, this is quite impossible to know, unless you interact with the person concerned.

In my understanding, these two aspects of our life hold equal, or in some cases more importance than physical well-being alone. This is because these are the two aspects which get bruised, battered daily and in some cases hit so hard that it is beyond intelligence to repair these.

These mentally and emotionally unfit people walk among us every day. We interact with them unknowingly; and we start carrying their residual energies with us.

We react to these because that's what we do best. We stop believing in our outlook to life, but on the contrary fill our hearts with revenge and envy; give into feelings of superiority or even inferiority. All this comes down to carrying their mental virus just to pass it on to another.

To hold 'fort' of your 'self', prevent it from unseen attacks which unbalance you and makes you mentally and emotionally unwell to take 'effort'.

Just as you eat right and exercise right to gain physical health. One must review their daily actions before going to sleep. Take time out, make peace in your heart; pray and look forward for a new sunrise free from all negativities! ”

Much love

The Awakening of the Sacred

"It is good to be a rational person. It is good to weigh pros and cons before making a decision. But we all do that, don't we? And still most of us are not happy with the outcomes.

Maybe, if given a second chance we would know what road to choose. But wait. At that juncture, at that point in our lives, we 'had' weighed the outcome and therefore chose the road accordingly!

It is said and practiced by many a saint that the time to evolve spiritually happens only at major junctures of one's life, and only when the path you choose at that specific time is not for personal gain but for a greater good.

For the personal choice eventually leads to more personal choices to seek happiness like a never ending egoistical carrousel. Realize at that point that you are but just a catalyst for the spirit of God to do its work through you, and experience the greatest joy of basking in the shadow of God's love from thereon!

The personal 'self' will never experience that which is sacred. It is only 'that' which is sacred in your being which awakens to its true identity."

Much love

Event Horizon

"Everything at one point will be taken away from you. And it is a fact known to those who see the world as it is without the veil of illusion blinding their sight.

And to this above point I elaborate.

Things come our way 'before', just for it to be taken away at some point in our life. Youth, money, health; maybe even a person with whom you have developed a close bond.

And many a times it works the other way around too – finding new love, unexpected windfall of money; a cure for a health condition etc. The point therefore is to specify that everything around you even 'you' included is just an 'Event' which is ever changing within its horizon.

Let go of any fixed notions of life therefore. How bad can bad be? And how good can good be? Your eternal self will continue to exist in some form or the other. This universe is ever changing, and you too are a part of the ever changing energy of the universe. Be happy for even the universe is incomplete without your existence."

Much love

The Defining Moment of Change

"The coming of change... would you ever accept it? Or would you hold on to your ritualistic patterns where you thrive in comfort?

Change is always met with caution and sometimes ridicule because it compels us to deal with a very realistic matrix of thought provoking concepts!

I know I am changing every second... and this change is also for the better because my old ideologies are either being validated or being eradicated from my consciousness!

Fear not the winds of change in your life I say... For change always brings a basket full of fresh new experiences for you to grow in spirit."

Much love

The Protective Clothing

"Ever felt worn out? Tired of everything? Exhausted beyond words? And wondered if it's the cause of your physical ill-health?

Well in all probability it's never just your physical state of being.

For even to feel physically well one has to feel well from within first.

Your thoughts, your emotions will heal first and always then the physical self will follow.

So sometimes to wear protective clothing means to just protect your emotions and thoughts for these two are always under your control.

Read good books, interact with positive people, even watch movies and tv shows which leave you with a 'positive' feel good factor.

You will be in the pink of physical health!"

Much love

The Enclosure of Fear

"This crazy feeling of total fear stems out of believing in everything and anything.

Why not investigate for yourself, maybe what you have heard could be gossip, loose talk, someone else's insecurities or even someone knowing that you are an easy person to spook is having fun at your expense.

Use discretion, logic and intelligence in times like these.

And avoid passing information to another unless you have filtered it. Be wise, you are capable of being so!"

Fear not! Much love!

Two Sides of the Coin

"It is in the EGO where grudges find shelter and it is in simplicity where forgiveness roots itself.

For it is the EGO which evaluates and measures every deed done by another and it is the Humility in oneself which gently encourages you to do a good deed for nothing in return.

Humility and forgiveness are the two sides of the same coin and both these attributes belong to your higher self, 'That' self which will eventually awaken through the trials of your life."

Much love

The Elusive Future

"In this dynamic ever changing world we live in, where situations change faster than your reactionary capabilities, it's foolish to think you will know the outcome of any situation unfolding.

Stop trying to predict the future therefore; the whole exercise is futile.

The NOW you live in, the NOW you breathe is where reality has rooted itself. No matter what your situation is find your happiness in the NOW. Setting goals for future happiness is literally like chasing your own shadow, no matter how fast you run to catch it your shadow will always elude you.

Take in this moment for this moment also belongs to you and your happiness."

Much love

Assumptions

"I take time to understand the other, for I wish not to be misunderstood myself.

'Assumptions' are what we carve out in our minds about another person's persona! And misunderstanding's always stem from these very assumptions.

Be patient in dealing with others. Refrain from character assassination of a person, for all you know the person in question might really not be as 'bad' as you imagined.

Forming assumptions about others based on little or no direct interaction with the person is a way of taking on a great amount of 'Negative' energy!

Spare yourself from the negative energy, give that someone one more chance, for all you know you might just embark on a fantastic journey of friendship and/or Love! Spread the joy."

Much love

Preparedness

"Preparedness... to be willing to accept that anything, anytime, anywhere can go wrong or not as you expected and you still have the required tools to fix it!

But this preparedness I wish to imply on people we trust and people we love.

We seldom expect a loved one's attitude change towards us or a trusted friend or family member let us down where trust issues are concerned. But what if the unimaginable does happen to you! Do you have the tools to fix the relationship in question?

I therefore like to view a relationship purely on strengths of compassion and forgiveness from my perspective.

Do I have it in me to forgive and forgo the issue and still welcome the person in my life? If so, then I have achieved the ability to love without condition. A non conditional love is a doorway to your higher self. It is a tool of preparedness, it is a deterrent of a selfish personality.

Love without bounds for YOU deserve it!"

Much love

The Purpose

"If you must include 'Purpose' in the dictionary of your life then do so with utmost care for 'Purpose' by itself is your inner inertia. It is a power to mould your thinking and activate a self taught belief in anything.

Against this backdrop of an illusionary world and time, your purpose of existence is nothing more than beginning a 'Quest' for the ultimate truth.

Which is... where were you before you were born and where will you be when physical death claims you?

This purpose if left un-questioned would be living a lie on purpose."

Much love

Transformation Into Pure Consciousness

"What is it about our minds that functions solely on logic and rational thinking? All I see the mind do is calculate and calculate everything... Even life!

If we have to put life in an algebraic equation it would seem like this :-

Amount of years to live = X
Expense per year = Y
Average inflation per year = % ?

(X) x (Y) x (%) = (Money required in the bank).

This would be the perfect bank balance to achieve. Then, a comfortable life would follow. But until then it's an uphill struggle.

But in reality we don't have knowledge of things to come. Maybe a breakthrough in the field of science and technology where physical death might be an option and not an eventuality.

What if you were to live beyond the years you thought and that to in the pink of health? And I am not speaking just 50 or 100 years more... How about 500 or more! It's just impossible to even think about it. But what if? Would the things which make a difference in your life today be the same then? The random events which take you by surprise today and stress you out completely, apply then?

If you manage to get your hands on some scientific facts and breakthroughs you will realize that mankind has taken humongous leaps in science and technology in just the last 100 years.

Buckle up then for what awaits us in just a few years from today is something which even your mind will shy away from probing.

For this world is not designed by logic and mind but by a consciousness. This shift from logical thinking to consciousness awakening is what is taking place.

Every aspect of you is going through changes and that which mattered today will not matter then, for your perspective will be that of a higher being by itself. A being far superior to a logical thinking brain. ”

Much love

The Gift

"Giving gifts are a part of many cultures. The give and take of gifts was practiced long ago as an expression of love. 'We' in all we do today, also love receiving gifts, gifts of material nature.

That unexpected gift! That receiving something, anything from someone leaves us with a very positive sense of well-being. But as we start indulging more in this practice without understanding the essence behind the gift the material gift by itself becomes more important than the essence of what it's meant to carry.

Similarly, in a broader sense we never equate our life as a 'Gift' from God. We start equating our life with mundane activities, unimportant issues and sometimes failed relationships or careers start giving into feelings of unsuccessfulness, depression or failures forgetting the essence of life completely.

What is the essence of life? If I were to sum it up in one word it would be 'Appreciation'. Thank you God for the Gift of Life."

Much love

The Faltered Mindset

"Most intelligent people work backwards, relying on past experiences and past statistics. Major decisions are based on these principles. Almost everything they do or even think of doing arises from a particular past.

Eg: Because a short dark man in the past with a mustache stole my bread, all short dark men with mustache's are not to be trusted.

This is the basis of how the intelligent mind generalizes and in doing so actually blocks pure spiritual knowledge which is being piled up just outside your limited mindset waiting for you to welcome it.

One of the greatest reasons on why you can't see the workings of God is purely because of this faltered mindset it's habit of generalizing past events, making you believe that the solution to everything is text book science. Maybe the argument is 'That's the way the mind works', but in all reality the limitations of the mind, is where we have confined our existence in.

The direct beaming of spiritual knowledge and the unlocking of finer spiritual dimensions comes with just stopping to generalize everything about your experiences.

You are unique and so are your life experiences. The hidden meanings and teachings are for you and you alone. Search the spiritual principal behind each event of your life be it good or bad but welcome this direct communication with God daily."

Much love

Synthesizing Harmony

"Maybe I am wrong, wrong in my perspective entirely, but how am I to know? For if anyone suggests an alternative I am capable of beating them with my arguments completely. You see I have the gift of the gab or so I believe.

But some have managed to win arguments just by intimidating me by raising their voices or displaying irrational behaviour. So I conclude it's a method I must adopt to forward my ways of asserting my arguments based on my perspective, but again how am I to know if I am wrong?

It is said for sensibilities to see light; a harmonious existence is a must.

Look back at history; it has always been in times of peace where culture, art and knowledge have flourished.

Arguments, irrational behaviour, intimidation are actually a hindrance for genuine good to come about in our own personal environment.

Your home and your work environment is where you have to synthesize harmony completely. By believing, just believing in the productiveness of the outcome it offers. This should motivate you enough to seek it.

So your questions of whether you are wrong or right will not apply, as your own harmonious existence would have begun to guide you and your decisions all along. Remember a peaceful existence is the only way to achieving the first phase of happiness. ”

Much love

The Debt

"All of us, each one of us who walks this earth does so because of a great burden of debt with certain people. Call it karma if you must but people who we are connected to, without our own independent choice, all fall in this category.

They are our grandparents, parents our brothers sisters and our children.

We will never understand why fate chose them for us but if you pay close attention you will come to realize that, these are the very same people in our lives whom we have expectations from and the pain which arises when our expectations are not met sometimes is not easy to digest or forget!

God has chosen a certain network of these very people to walk with us. The disharmony caused by our expectations, fragment the smooth inter-winding of feelings with them causing an inner unbalance, which in turn affects our personalities.

Expect less from this network of people. Reduce your pain by doing so, for all you know they too have expectations from you which have not been met and are silently in pain too.

Harmonize this network for its a God given design for you to work on. Every negative thought about them must be addressed first, neutralized and eventually harmonized for its the long time overdue debt which must be cleared first. ”

Much Love

The Purity of Passion

"Let monetary gain not be the reason of your passion, for your passion is in itself a bright spot in your circle of creativity.

This passion has to find its way to work on all levels of your personality so as to uplift your consciousness in its entirety by putting a price to what you love doing is actually dimming the bright spot.

Do what you love. Follow your heart, your passion. You will find grace in doing so and remember the byproduct of passion is always success and success can always translate to monetary or spiritual gain."

Much love

Reason Your Way to Harmony

"We all have reasons to do things we do... and this reasoning is also sometimes the cause of great pain to ourselves and others.

I always say to such individuals that if you have eaten just one slice of a pizza why did you order the whole pizza?

In other words the reasoning of your pain should not just stop at the 'problem discovered', but instead go for the extra inch of understanding, ask yourself why is it there in the first place! And next, how do I make this problem go away...

I consider people who discover problems as self attested negative individuals! Because they tend to 'stop' reasoning at the discovery of the problem and start 'reacting' to it. The incomplete circle is like a half eaten pizza... One has to eat the whole pizza while it is hot and tasty! You have to reason further and arrive at solutions not just react to it!

So if problem is discovered, you need to move to 'Problem understood', and finally to the solution...and don't you love it when you hear 'No problem señor!'"

Much love

The Mental Commotion

"A night so silent... Where has all the commotion gone? Asleep they say... Asleep...

A mind that can quieten as the envelop of darkness blankets the day sky; is surely not above the universal events which govern the workings of this world.

Our infallible attitude towards the workings of this world and our self imposed beliefs on ourselves and others is the actual cause of great grief and disharmony.

It is not in the minds capacity which will connect the missing link of harmony and happiness in this world. It is; and will arguably be the reason for grief and disharmony.

Your mind is an understanding unfolding within its own realities. Trust not it completely for if you must achieve the desired harmony and happiness. It will surely be the all encompassing universe around you which will nudge you to it. Trust the infinite to bring you to it. Surrender to this infinite for it is already doing what it must for your consciousness development and let your mind sleep this illusionary slumber..."

Much love

The Shift to the Inner-Vision

"My physical eyes are the same,it has always been a part of me since my physical embodiment...

But what has changed and changed so much is the world which surrounds me...

My memory often takes me on a long and misty walk by that narrow winding path to my early days of my childhood, and thrusts me to remember what I visioned then, my aspirations, my dreams, my joys, my fears every bit of it...which are all but just a distant dream today. My childhood is long over, my adult life a static reality.

This static reality which I live by today, what I envision now, this aspiration, this dream, this joy and this fear would be a distant dream some day in my future too I am sure.

I want not to be blinded by this surrounding world, therefore I pray... and try to train these same physical eyes to envision this veil of illusion and the transitory effect of it...For by doing so it will awaken my inner-vision to the fluid reality behind this static world.

The inner-vision must be strengthened enough to focus on the ultimate truth, behind the illusion of physical death too...for life and consciousness exists very much beyond these unseen borders!"

Much love

The OGE

"Read it backwards and you have the word. I have carefully placed these letters backwards so the word itself does not command this message but instead your understanding about it does.

Everything about ourselves is rooted in this word. Your good side and your bad side, your perception of this world and also the retrospect of all your decisions in your life.

You will be experiencing inferiority or superiority complexes and you won't even be aware of it till you truly understand 'OGE'.

You are to put it in simpler terms, but a sum total of everything you have experienced in this life, what you might have read in books and also the people you have interacted with. So your 'OGE' has been quite a random act if looked upon plainly.

If one has to ask me what's the best definition of it, I would like to compare 'OGE' to a tempered glass where it doesn't crack in two but it shatters and still holds itself together. Ever noticed a windshield of a car? It's shattered to such tiny pieces that you can't see clearly through it... just the light shadows make it through...

That's exactly what happens to our thoughts and ideas, our convictions and our beliefs over a period of time, while living this life. Your 'OGE' like the tempered glass starts to shatter little by little...when your very beliefs and convictions are taken apart by your own life experiences only to be replaced by inferiority or superiority complexes.

Your nature has been formed accordingly and people around you are liking you if your ideologies match or disliking you if they don't.

So now after having understood that our 'OGE' is more a random outcome, how do we take control of it and start crafting our own 'EGO'?

Well it's not that difficult but you will have to work from a side of yours unknown to the 'OGE' that of 'HUMILITY'.

To humble oneself is to craft your 'EGO' It will be an act for the betterment of oneself and your loved ones.

Remember the path to restructure your entire personality is to humble yourself. ”

Much love

The Dynamic Power of Choice

"The world around us, tells us a new story everyday. Things may seem similar but their meanings change every time we interpret the happenings.

What is then 'dynamic' is our ability to interpret.

With this dynamic ability to read the same happenings differently, why do we falter and take a one dimensional view of our lives?

It is said and I believe it so, those who learn to work with a 'choice' on a daily basis are the ones who always chose to better their life each day.

For it is ultimately our choice — our choice on how we view the happenings around, our choice on how we view our relationship, our choice to be in the same mental state or not and our choice to snap out of bad habits!

So use your dynamic power of 'choice' to better your tomorrow and open your mind a bit more, to have a multiple view of the world around you."

Much love

The Hope

"In the little box of wishes, tucked away in your dreams...the most precious is 'Hope'.

To 'hope' is to seek a brighter tomorrow... To 'hope' is to reignite your passion...

To 'hope' is to rekindle faith once more... To 'hope' is to embrace love all over again.

And remember:-

Losing 'hope' means losing everything which makes you human. Losing 'hope' opens the floodgate to negativity.

Losing 'hope' is certifying your failure! Losing 'hope' is an act of cowardice in itself!

So be 'HOPEFUL' and in doing so, you shall transform into a wonderful person who will eventually bring 'Hope' to all the rest..."

Much love

The Analogy of 'Odds'

"I was parked at a traffic signal today waiting for the light to turn green when on the opposite side of the road a truck loaded with oranges just passed by over a speed braker and with the velocity it travelled and the momentum, the impact of the wheels on the speed braker made an orange, a single orange fly up and land smack in the middle of the road... Undamaged.

The orange was slowly rolling to the sidewalk as the road was slightly inclined... When more cars, trucks and motorcycles started zooming on that road I was sure the orange had no chance to make it and soon ants were going to have orange juice as breakfast. More than a hundred vehicles passed and nothing, absolutely 'nothing' happened to the orange.

The orange rolled to the curb and stayed there till an urchin who was begging near a traffic signal came and picked it up, peeled it and started eating it.

There are many ways to look at a simple incident like this but just applying a spiritual principal behind it changes everything about it. Here goes...

1. No matter how tough or hard life it may seem, your destiny is not governed by the obvious. Your fate is your precise timing of doing things and things happening to you because of it. Like the orange

rolling at a specific speed because of the shape and size it was, saved it from being squashed by oncoming traffic. Think about it, if it was larger or smaller the rolling speed of it would be different and therefore its fate, so no matter what information you may have gathered regarding your fears - 'it may not apply to you' you like the orange are rolling down a specific timeline designed only for you. And the traffic can be denoted as your fears.

2. The universe figured out a way to feed the urchin. Maybe his body required vitamin C. Which he was totally unaware of but none the less it was provided for him. We are just like the urchin we have been provided different forms of mental and emotional nourishment by the universe and are totally unaware of it... Therefore being complacent about it we seek only what we desire, but take away those things which actually give you the mental and emotional support and 'DESIRE' would just be a word from a dictionary having nothing to do with your life. Be grateful for the people in your life, they are there for a purpose too. ”

Much love

Spiritual Quotient Unplugged

"The world is designed in a way that forces one to compete to succeed, you have to be the best, better than the rest, and the secret is by being 'selfish' you will always gain an edge over the other.

But a selfish state of mind will only alienate one from another in the long run.

And this individualistic ability of climbing over others to reach the top and using all means under the garb of EQ and IQ to do it will eventually rob you of SQ!

Yes Spiritual Quotient is a force to reckon with. In this man made jungle where everything is pitched under the common umbrella of monetary gain and success, you have been robbed considerably of SQ.

Your pristine character, your space of mental and emotional balance, your ability to attract love, and your compassionate self are all a part of SQ.

So every once in a while do consider evaluating yourself from your spiritual quotient viewpoint. For in doing so you might just influence a whole lot of others who are connected to you, to find their SQ too."

Much love

The Destination

"So many mundane thoughts which fill my mind... So many real questions left unanswered... and so many daily miracles overlooked!

I walk this journey alone I know...for I have intently looked at the eyes of the other and found their destination elsewhere...

If we were to reason with our 'thoughts', if we were to 'seek' the questions left unanswered, and If we were to look at the 'miracles' happening around us daily... Maybe just maybe 'all' would seek the same destination collectively..."

Much love

The Revered Story Books

"Why I question... Why do you stand so committed to the reasoning of others!

Like a story book read out to an innocent child they convinced you about a tale once told...

But the essence of the story was to awaken your eternal reasoning and put you on the path to self discovery...

But the characters of the story is what played out in your mind... And the characters of the story is what you remembered.

Do read your story books once again and let the fragrance of the real spiritual truths find way in your 'own' reasoning."

Much love

The Symmetric Unfoldment of Truth

"There is a very powerful force within you... It is powering everything about you, even your brain. It is never what you think that makes you, it is 'What you make yourself think' that makes you!

Your thoughts are mostly never your own. In this wide array of information warfare through media, micro blogging with friends and popular beliefs, you indoctrinate yourself to a botched up attitude of self that is quite alienated from a truth which you carry within.

Understand the subtly, the fluidity, and the immense power of this force which powers your being in its entirety. Revere it too... Nothing, absolutely nothing can consume it or defeat it. It is eternal in its true sense. It is the real you. It is your 'Soul'.

View your world from the eyes of your soul and you will unlock the greatest truths about your eternal self! It is then that you will come to learn, even the sunset, was cast in the 'illusion' of a symmetric unfoldment meant only for your physical eyes. And time will literally stand still in the absorption of the genuine secret of creation which just unfolded for the eyes of your soul."

Much love

The Harmonious Existence

"It is in wonder that you seek an in-depth analysis to things which inspire you... There is no greater inspiration than 'love' by itself... Because of the various forms it presents itself in.

But the 'Love' which intrigues most of the human race is that of 'MAN and WOMAN' for which an understanding is required to put one on the path of contentment.

We seek love from another... But what we generally are seeking is 'Harmony', a perfect emotional balance through which a sense of overall well-being of an individual can be defined.

Each one of us is either carrying a male force or a female force within. And each force independently is a volatile when exposed to the opposite force a vibrational selection in your field of 'aura' selects the one who you automatically get 'attracted' to. This attraction is purely for your force to neutralize itself; to create harmony.

And when reciprocated you sense caring, kindness and compassion for the person, which are all the outcomes of 'Harmony' or what we call 'love' for the person.

A physical relationship should always be an extension of a harmonious relationship. Never seek it the other way round.

More later on this amazing subject called 'LOVE'. ”

Much love

Silence in Divinity

"It is the poetic silence which devoured the mental capability and taught the mind to believe in its own supremacy. Your EGO was born out of the 'Great Silence' of the supreme being or 'HE' who most of us refer to as 'God'.

It is in 'silence' therefore where you will find the true meaning of 'God'.

It is also in the same 'silence' where you will achieve the mastery over your mind.

Gift yourself some silence each day. It is after all the divine quality of the supreme being himself..."

Much love

Underneath the Starry Nights

"Lonely are the nights underneath these star covered skies. Where the wind blows in periodic silence to the tune of the hidden crickets...

Am I alone? I often wonder...for I ask, who at this moment in their deep slumber holds my thoughts?

This night like every other is a gentle reminder and a prime moment to realize that, every night these hours are gifted to me; to be alone by myself away from the rest. Call it sleep if you do...or use the paradigm shift of understanding that it is actually a time to connect with your true being...To be away from the chaotic world and a moment to realize your existence as a child of the cosmos underneath the very same starry nights."

Much love

Pebble in the Lake

"I picked up a pebble just to throw it deep in the lake. The ripples it formed reached my foot where I stood in the shallow water's. It happened slowly but surely...

This action had created a result it seemed and quite literally I like to think of the 'Great being' in the similar sense.

Our consciousness has been thrown like a pebble clothed in a physical body in this great 'existence' or call it the ocean of cause and effect and like ripples on the water, the ups and downs, the good and the bad we will weather on this return journey home.

Similarly we will be reaching his heavenly grace little by little and our consciousness will touch his feet, his heavenly grace slowly but surely.

Throw a pebble into a lake today and visualize this truth yourself..."

Much love

Breaking Down the Stone Wall

"The greatest emotional burden one carries is the one caused by oneself. That part of you which puts all 'Trust and Faith' in another. It is always a trusting heart which gets broken. All your emotional pain if evaluated will find its root cause in your trusting self!

To rid yourself of this emotional burden is never easy, but it is a requirement for a more loving and enriched life.

A pen and paper always works best for once you write it down you visit that sensitive part of your experience. You re-live it and in doing so you start understanding yourself bit by bit. And at a point of recounting you will enter a viewpoint where you blame no one, not even yourself. Let the silence of that moment absorb you and that is the point of healing.

The dark energy of resentment, the propagated ideologies of guilt... Those shades of living your life as the one who was victimized are all meaningless, for you create a stone wall around your true self. That 'self' which is the only part of yourself capable of receiving pure love from the creator himself..."

Much love

A Lesson in Humility

"The most difficult, the most controversial and the most misunderstood thing is to find humility.

Because no one really knows the true meaning of it, or what it can do for oneself...

So to the above I elaborate...Finding 'Humility' within oneself opens doors to the infinite cosmos and the unseen 'God worlds', knowledge of self, your eternal being is what gets realized.

'Humility' is an art which is the first lesson taught by the learned spiritual masters to the new seekers and it has to be tracked independently and daily.

There is one exercise which I like to share, it's says to hold a constant thought that - 'The other people are nicer than me' and even though all your reasoning may refute it, the actual build of 'Humility' will begin at this step. For there is the unseen wall of ego which surrounds you, which gives you a sense of control, your intelligence forms a part of it too blocking all types of higher information which is just out of your awareness area. This wall of ego crumbles as humility within oneself sets in and in doing so the light of your true spiritual self starts to shine through like the rays of the sun simmering on the morning dew found on rose petals...

Here is where the equilibrium of your awareness comes in tune with your higher self...

Try this method, remember that the path of awakening the eternal is always through the internal. ”

Much love

The Doorway to Dimensions

"It moves just as it flows, we live in a state which eventually changes, and then we carry the experience with us always to the next dimension.

It is called 'memory' or that 'what' makes us... It is this part of you which records the experience, the good and the painful too.

But the painful memories are a more powerful force, as they are always coupled with the emotional wounds. And therefore have an ability to attach their talons deep in our consciousness.

What really makes one take in the whole new experience of change and welcome the infinite force of the spirit around us is, when you walk into the new dimension with a free heart... a light self, free of fears and carrying no emotional burden...

Practice the art of letting go of the residual pain of previous experiences daily. You were born free of all the emotional complexities and fears and that's how you will enter and absorb the true God Worlds too.

Even this moment now, is as beautiful and divine as the future of your infinite existence and if it is being marred it is only by the residual forces of your deep rooted painful experiences or fears."

Much love

The Independent Stride

"Most people don't know it but are still reeling under a great pressure called 'Dependency'.

Yes I do agree that 'Dependency' is the basic fabric of societies and cultures, of marriages and relationships, of families and your group of friends... But in this very nature of being dependent we find 'Comfort' and in doing so we delay the walk of an 'Independent' stride.

As time progresses and moves in the forward direction you are quite simply left alone, for many of your people including dependable people would have moved ahead along the same timeline to experience what waits for them.

Being independent starts at the 'Thought' level — before you agree or disagree on any thought of others evaluate it yourself and being independent emotionally starts at a 'Compassionate' level. For if you can't feel another's emotional pain how can you realize yours and overcome it?

Be dependent if you wish to, it's a great way to enjoy human interaction. But do realize that the gift of life was a 'spiritual one' and to realize it would entail being independent — emotionally and mentally."

Much love

The Breath of Life

"If I have felt close to an unseen force, that which has always mystified my existence is solely because I have seen through the seen forces of my life!

It's been said in so many ways and yet the illusion has blinded every human eye...

You are and will always be at his mercy. It is a power so great, so mightily immense that every breath of your life and the life of your loved ones is because of his grace... His will...

Breath in his precious love... Breath out his worthy praise... Glorify your existence by this itself... He deemed you fit to be blessed with life and therefore you have no right to think anything less about yourself...or others too!"

Much love

The 'Caring' Self

"Spiritually speaking, 'Is it important to care for people, who don't care about you?'

Breaking this question down in the 'worldly' sense the answer is a sure negative, but place this under the spiritual viewpoint...and the whole meaning of this question changes...

For the day one finds the answer to this question he would have realized much more about himself than he could ever conceive.

For to 'Care' is to look into the heart of another. Before the whimper of pain can echo the soothing balm of love and understanding would have dressed their emotional wounds. This person in question even if he turned his back to you after you would have healed him, would have left you with a great gift of understanding compassion.

And after you experience 'Compassion' in its true sense you will be incapable of turning your back to 'compassion' itself! The walk of spiritual discovery opens a multitude of doors within your being. 'Being Caring' is just one of them..."

Much love

The Bond

Your emotional bonding should never be to a point of your vulnerabilities...

If you must, do try and strengthen these very same friendships and relationships by carrying your own emotional burden...

Much love

The Passion of the Seeker

"Passion is not about getting the job done, it's about perfecting it.

If this similar principal was to be applied to our higher self, that self which is the seeker in all of us, then we would never stop at the illusion of the exterior world which we all are a part of.

We would seek further into the depths of creation, we would seek further into the depths of love, we would seek further into the chambers of knowledge.

Awaken the passion of your seeker within the 'Job' of entering this existence is already done with!"

Much love

A Memory of Sorts

"All that binds or repels is memory and memory by itself disintegrates when an external superior force is applied upon.

Every molecule is a memory in its form...the gravitational force and the magnetic force of the earth too.

It is memory which keeps the planet and it's satellites in orbit spinning for billions of years.

Similarly, your life is a compilation of events which are structured into a memory format...even your desires form a part of it!

The great external force (God) can rip apart all my memories by a single stroke, and illuminate my being with pure knowledge. But it chooses to love like no other by layering my memory with more events.

Thus forcing me to find a way out...and in doing his 'will' I improve my memory and redefine my uniqueness.

The amount of perfection in this universe is mind numbing...just putting your thoughts on this alone is opening your memory into another dimension!"

Much love

A Seeker of Perfection

"I fear no mistakes... I pay no heed to advice for I envision perfection first. It's the mistakes which drive me to realign myself and at every step of realignment I perfect 'That' what is best for me!

I am fearless today or so I believe, wandering in the unknown pathways of life. There are hardships once the sun sets, I know for darkness itself can swallow the faith of any man.

No I will not light the torch of faith... Not yet... Not now for I have to first learn to see in darkness too."

Much love

An Atheist Approach

"If the conflict is there, the solution is too.

What really hides itself and makes the conflict last longer than required is the 'EGO' of man.

Every conflict has its root cause in its ideologies which were proposed at some point and it's these very ideologies which are defended, politicized or enforced.

But if one were to ask, what's the required ideology to attain the understanding of self and God? It would be first defining the workings of the EGO which hides behind these very ideologies and makes you think within the enclosure of this superficial spherical dome.

Every 'thought', be it right or wrong, should be open for debate for only then will the hidden EGO come into the foray.

A real seeker is also an atheist it is said, for he dared to question the unimaginable, 'Who created God?'

And in doing so he just opened a debate, and the fallout of this debate was ironic for he got branded as an 'Atheist'.

Define your Ego first, take whatever road you must, for you must know someday, 'Why do you think the way you do?'

The day you do 'define' yourself the magical will happen and true freedom will be within your human grasp. ”

Much love

The Camouflaged Greed

"You want and want and want for more and then you ask for a little more...just a little more. Then you strive for some more till 'more' becomes you.

What is it about greed that we can't see? It is that it has taken the identical shape of us. The 'More' within us camouflaged in the garb of ambition.

Yes go on; fulfill your dreams. 'Everyone must' but when the outcomes of your struggle are met with unprecedented failures remember it's the 'More' within you which is crying out the pain!

Let it be, recognize it, for the true voice of success is always a harmonious interlink between your dreams and your conviction and it resonates as constant happiness too in the face of failures!

For in reality we all are truly above the events and forces which are at play in this world... And this we know and recognize it in our own moment of solitude and silence."

Much love

Eggs in a Basket

"In India we pride ourselves with something called 'Doorstep services'; every commodity you can imagine at your doorstep... One such incident I'd like to share with you'll.

My local bread and eggs delivery man religiously comes everyday at a fixed time to my house and rings the bell delivering the much required supplies. I noticed how he carries the delicate items and suggested an alternative to him by which the eggs would be safe while he transports them on his old rusted bicycle.

Imagine carrying over 360 eggs in a jute bag over the handle bar of his cycle; one and it's disaster.

He smiled and said 'Sir it's because of the way I carry them that I am careful while cycling all the way here. The day I get comfortable I might get reckless and then for sure I would lose more than just the eggs.'

I was amazed at his insight and the spiritual lesson he left behind with me. Are problems and difficulties in life a way God keeps us in check? Knowing that if he comforts us sooner than required it might just be disastrous for our spiritual growth...

Whatever you may conclude is not that important. What is, is the ability to learn life's lessons from the most unassuming teachers."

Much love

The Build of Character

"He had an opinion about everything but decided on nothing! He waited to see which way the crowd went and then took centre stage to proclaim a known lie that he was the 'first' to make the decision! Recognize these individuals, they are amongst us, might even be within us.

Character building starts with making decisions, not just having empty opinions and discussions about the trivial issues which influence our lives.

So make a 'decision' today no matter what the outcome. And experience your inner strength grow, which will eventually gift you with the brightest jewel called 'Character'.

For only when you walk the path would you know the pathways."

Much love

The Secret of Enlightenment

"The great ocean of mankind is tuned to a life that their predecessors have passed on to them...every emotion, every thought and belief has found a name in this dictionary of life.

How different can 'different' be then? For one will always belong to one side of any given equation and the 'difference' if one were to question, is first finding that uniqueness in yourself.

Search for a 'THOUGHT' in your mind which doesn't belong to the outside universe of interaction. That unique thought, whatever it may be should not even be the seed of another ones thought; it is this purity that is the first insight of your own self, your own creative self that 'thought' it is said, is what will inspire you to seek further unique thoughts, and eventually put you on the path to enlightenment.

The language of pure spirit, the source of enlightenment, doesn't belong to any known language. It transcends through the unknown and submerges itself into your 'being', makes you one with the infinite; empowered with a fountain of pure love for eternity."

Much love

A Change of Heart

"Friendships and relationships are bound by the thinnest of cords magnetized by emotions all the way.

Negative episodes in one's life weaken these cords. But it's never out of a reactionary outcome, it's more out of personal choice.

The affected use this negative flow of energy to read into friendships and relationships, evaluating microscopic details about them. Being in a negative zone, the only thing they pick up or understand is, the 'negativity' of these very same friendships and relationships. Eventually, these individuals push themselves into solitude, self pity and sometimes experience a complete sense of superiority.

Either way they alienate themselves from the others in question. Whatever the outcome, the cord is forcefully broken.

Look around I say, every person in your life will eventually break that cord with you within this universal time, so don't challenge time yet, these relationships and friendships are a great gift of love from the creator, cherish the people in your life.

Remember time flows faster than thought! So forgive all of them and in doing so, alleviate your own pain."

Much love

The Character

"Let it be, let's not judge another's 'character' as while we do, we open up ourselves to the moral law, of being judged to by the same, who we had an opinion on or passed a moral judgment on.

Everybody has a right to have an opinion but to influence another so as to propagate your own beliefs is basically a sign of a morally weak person by itself."

Much love

Universe Knows Best

"The start of a valuable relationship always comes when the person does not match up to your expectations and you still can't find the reason why you are still with the person. It's here where the connection 'has' already taken place. You'll have joined each other's universe. This is done with the grace which we shall call 'The Spirit'. Now from here on, the real training or working out your karma begins; because the universe knows why it has chosen you both to cross each other's path.

Now I know there are also many who will ask, what about those who came in our lives and have gone away? Maybe, even we might have left someone and moved on to new or other relationships. Again, the forces of the universe are working in complete unison with us, even if we are or aren't aware of this.

Every relation you have as of now has a deeper meaning behind it, for either we are gaining experience or learning valuable lessons from them or they from us. It also could be that we are becoming the catalyst for them to meet other people as 'The Universe Knows Best'.

We call it matters of the heart, affection, love but still one must be aware that every relation you will have with any person whatever the outcome, the end result is to fine tune your energy levels for the greater knowledge, 'God Knowledge' to flow into you, it is to prepare you to experience the greatest love for you to open up to so as to understand it, to bring it in your consciousness, to make this universal love a part of your being. So much a part of you that eventually, it will fill you up and flow 'outward' through you in this world.

So be 'in love', work out your differences in your relationships, with whoever the universe has chosen for you...it could be your lover, your spouse, your child, your neighbour, your boss, your employee or just a nagging 'nobody'. Universal love is finding its way to enter you, so don't hold back.

Work towards harmony, in whichever way you deem possible, find the peace, and find the balance for this universe has already embraced you for eternity. ”

Much love

Complexities

"Try and achieve the difficult, but when you do, remember the world around will be least impressed. For they envision their capabilities much superior to your own.

I have known a few, who walk this life with complexities of their superior attitude towards everything that they consider the world around them a bunch of fools.

Complexities of a superior nature is actually the fuel of negativity. All genuine failures of life stem from this one complexity, if viewed from another perspective.

Even if you feel you are the most intelligent or have the maximum emotional intelligence or might even be the most charitable person; to escape this monster which is known as a 'superiority complex' is most difficult to many. For it is 'that' which makes you look down upon people. Those people who may have more charity in their hearts, more love in their being or even more gratitude to God as compared to you.

Keep yourself in check therefore, as genuine success is always considered, when you win the hearts of people not when you set out to prove your superiority."

Much love